# TANKS

# TANKS

## THE TANKS OF THE WORLD IN 500 GREAT PHOTOS

Christopher Foss

This edition first published in 2003 by Crestline, an imprint of
MBI Publishing Company, Galtier Plaza, Suite 200,
380 Jackson Street, St. Paul, MN 55101-3885 USA

© Salamander Books Ltd., 2003

A member of **Chrysalis** Books plc

MBI Publishing Company books are also available at discounts
in bulk quantity for industrial or sales-promotional use.
For details write to Special Sales Manager at Motorbooks
International Wholesalers & Distributors, Galtier Plaza,
Suite 200, 380 Jackson Street, St. Paul, MN 55101-3885 USA.

ISBN 0-7603-1500-0

Designed and edited by:
FOCUS PUBLISHING, 11a St Botolph's Road, Sevenoaks,
Kent, England TN13 3AJ
Editors: Guy Croton; Vanessa Townsend
Designer: Philip Clucas MSIAD

Salamander editor: Anthony Shaw

Printed and bound in China

# Contents

# Introduction

The tank first appeared on the battle field during the First World War, but was not initially a success, as the vital breakthrough it made was not always supported by the following infantry. In the interwar period, some countries relegated the role of the tank to mainly infantry support or reconnaissance. This led to the development and fielding of either well armed but slow tanks, or very light tanks armed with machine guns which had poor levels of protection. Although there were officers in France, Britain, and the USA who clearly understood the concept of mobile warfare, it was Germany who perfected the tactics of using armor, infantry, artillery, and aviation assets to rapidly overcome any opposition.

Tanks built in Germany were superior until the arrival of the Russian T-34, late in 1941. While inferior to their German counterparts in many respects—especially in terms of armor and firepower—British and American tanks could be produced in large numbers, and in the end it was quantity and not quality that counted.

In the Cold War period, large fleets of what are now called Main Battle Tanks (MBTs) were fielded, which had significant improvements in the areas of armor, firepower, and mobility over earlier generation vehicles. The end of the Cold War has meant that MBT fleets have been drastically reduced in Europe, and some countries hope to replace them in the future by new systems that have similar capabilities but can be transported more rapidly by air.

This book comprises more than 500 pictures of tanks. Some of these are very well known—such as the Tiger, Panther, T-34, Churchill, and Sherman—but some lesser known and experimental vehicles have also been included. It does not pretend to be a complete record of every tank ever built.

**Opposite:** The impact of an anti-tank weapon hitting a target tank on a range is devastating. Such a hit would result in the death of all tank crew members.

In the history of warfare, weapons come and go. Yet since the Middle Ages there have been many attempts to produce war machines that would somehow be invulnerable to an enemy while being able to progress undisturbed around a battlefield, dispensing harm to all enemies in its path.

Until relatively recently (in historical terms), none of these optimistic projects could ever get past the drawing stage for the simple reason that the technology to build, power, and utilize such aggressive machines did not yet exist. But that did not stop numerous military philosophers from adding to the list of unlikely proposals.

**Above:** Known as "Little Willie", this was the first prototype of an armored track-laying vehicle. Note the tracks made from metal plates.

**Left:** US Army M1 Abrams main battle tanks pictured here on a Cold War exercise in Germany. First production M1s were armed with a 105mm gun, which was later upgraded and fitted with a 120mm gun.

It was only with the advent of the internal combustion engine that those old dreams could be transformed into reality. Relatively compact steam-driven or petrol-driven mechanical units could then replace the power of the vulnerable horse or human muscle. By the beginning of the 20th century, the internal combustion engine had emerged as being suitable for numerous applications by all manner of potential users—steam showed itself to be of little military utility, other than for tractors. Among the many possible applications for internal combustion were combat vehicles.

From about 1900 to 1914, there were many attempts to yoke the internal combustion engine to some kind of military role. Exactly what that role would be would exercise the minds of many military pundits for decades, so it is not too surprising that many of the early attempts to produce military vehicles were less than successful.

But almost without their designers understanding what they were accomplishing, they were laying the foundations of combat vehicle technology that were to develop to a remarkable extent until the present day. Yet in the history of warfare, that development period has been squeezed into less than a century.

Three main elements were to emerge as essential for a successful mobile combat machine—firepower, mobility, and protection. Like a three-legged stool, these elements had to balance to produce a satisfactory end product. Neglecting or over-emphasizing any one of the three would (and still will) inevitably result in a less than satisfactory solution when put to the acid test of combat. Many of the early attempts to produce some form of mobile combat machine floundered on at least two of the principles, if not all three.

It was appreciated early on that a measure of armor protection would be necessary for the vehicle involved to

**Right:** A British Mk I (male) in France on September 25, 1916. The wheels at the back were meant to assist steering, but were instead found to be redundant and were consequently removed.

survive on any battlefield. The usual early approach was to cover a conventional motor vehicle with steel or armored plates, or at least its most vulnerable parts. Very often the protection did not extend to the driver or other occupants, somewhat negating the original intention. Armament was at best limited to machine guns. For mobility, nearly all the early military vehicle attempts relied on wheels, and thin-rimmed wheels at that. While such vehicles might have been able to travel on roads or firm going, progress off-road was usually not possible or severely limited.

So while early experiments usually managed to provide some form of protection, they fell down when it came to mobility and firepower. Such shortcomings were usually combined with little idea of what military role the end product was meant to assume. The novelty of producing a

**Above:** The rear view of a British male Mk I tank. It differed from the female only in the armament.

mobile weapon platform was usually enough for the individuals involved, but the military of the day almost universally thought otherwise, pointing to the already-available mobility and firepower of the cavalry. Innovations such as complicated, expensive, and breakdown-prone military motor vehicles were thus thought unnecessary, and very few early innovators were given much encouragement.

Yet the seeds had been sown. Some pioneers persevered, so when the First World War broke out in 1914, the armored car had progressed one generation further forward than the early experimental vehicles, to the point where numbers were grudgingly absorbed into the ranks alongside the horse. Exactly what their military function was meant to be was still obscure, although ideas of using them for

**Above:** A captured Mk IV, with newly added German markings, leads an attack in the First World War.

reconnaissance or supporting cavalry operations were mooted and even attempted.

Once the First World War had settled down to trench warfare, there was little those early armored cars could accomplish. Events and conditions soon demonstrated that they lacked viable protection—their chassis and bodies were too flimsy for rough conditions, while their machine gun armament could rarely be used to any advantage. Gradual development would eradicate many of the armored cars' shortcomings, but they could not join in trench warfare. Armored cars did give good service in other parts of the world, such as the Middle East.

By 1915 trench warfare on the Western Front had been reduced to a stalemate. Any attempts by infantry to cross the churned terrain between the trench lines failed under hails of machine gun and massed rifle fire—and this, after encountering barbed wire obstacles. Yet the senior officers of the day could see little alternative to massing more and more soldiers into an attack and preceding this by ever-growing artillery barrages. Every time this was followed, the consequence was abject failure, combined with unbearable casualties.

Some means of breaking through the trench lines had to be found. The solution, when it came, had already been foreseen by a few, but they experienced little support for their efforts. The key was placing an armored internal combustion-engine powered hull onto caterpillar tracks of the type already in widespread use for agricultural and other commercial purposes. Armament could then be added. Getting such a combination to work under Western Front conditions demanded a period of

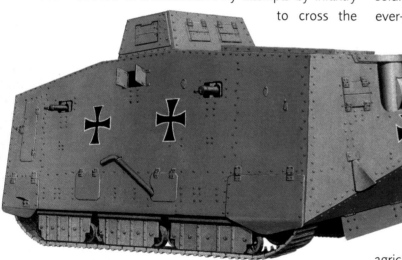

**Above:** A second version A7V with a 57mm gun in the front-plate, two 7.9mm machine guns each side, and one in the rear.

vehicles, the fact remains that the first such vehicle was produced in the UK. This was the "Little Willie" Landship of 1915, the progenitor of all that was to follow. "Little Willie" demonstrated that a possible trench warfare counter had been devised, but it still took time for the first vehicles, christened tanks as an innocuous cover

**Left, and below:** Conditions in the First World War battlefield were horrendous for the British Mk II (male) tanks (left). Towing weaponry out of the mud became commonplace (below).

development not assisted by a lack of foresight on the part of many military decision-makers. Gradually the challenges presented by using tracks to impart traction while spreading the load of a heavy superstructure were satisfactorily solved and initial objections were overcome.

## Early Days

Although there were numerous suggestions from many countries regarding the shape of future armored

**Right:** A camouflaged British Mk IV waits to join the attack during the Battle of Polygon Wood on September 26, 1917.

**Above:** Encountering tanks for the first time on the battlefield, German troops in the First World War try to maneuver captured British Mk IVs.

During 1917, there was a majority of serving officers who continued to regard the tank as a gimmick, their misgivings all too often reinforced by the tanks being asked to do more than their limited capabilities allowed them to accomplish. Yet, thanks to the persistence of officers who managed to grasp the potential of the tank, by the end of 1918 the tank had arrived as a viable military weapon, even if misunderstandings persisted among many.

name, to appear on the Western Front battlefields. Still imperfect due to frequent mechanical breakdowns, the first Mk I tanks, lumbering and slow vehicles, appeared on the Somme battlefields in late 1916. From then onwards, tanks began to carve a tactical niche for themselves as trench-crossing infantry support vehicles.

By 1918 tanks had also appeared in other nations'l hands. France, Germany, and Russia produced their own rudimentary tank designs with a view to employing them for infantry support, most designs being noteworthy for their sedate performance and modest armament. However, by 1918 the tank concept had already

diversified into self-propelled artillery and front-line personnel or supply carriers. Armored bridgelayers, combat engineer, and amphibious tanks were also in the early development stage. It seemed that the tank was to

**Right:** After the First World War, Germany was banned from producing tanks, so various names and guises were given to them, including "heavy tractors." This is a production line for PzKpfw V (Exp) tanks in 1935.

assume a new mantle—that of being a combat platform in its own right.

A few far-sighted military prophets had already forecast this concept. They foresaw that the tank could, in co-operation with that other novel war machine—the airplane—be employed to break through enemy lines, and then spread out to disrupt the enemy's rear areas and supply lines to reduce the enemy's ability to fight. There were British plans to introduce such tactics during 1919, but as the Armistice of November 1918 intervened those plans were never implemented. After 1918 the Great War armies faded away, and as they faded so did the funding and support needed to further develop the late 1918 proposals and the tank itself.

## Inter-war

For nearly two decades after 1918, very little of any significance happened regarding tank development. It

**Above:** A line of late Renault FT-17 light tank production models. Standard production models were armed with a 37mm gun, as opposed to a Hotchkiss 8mm machine gun.

remained regarded as an infantry support vehicle, a categorization that did much to stifle what little tank development did take place. Some desultory development, dependent on limited funding, did take place in several countries regarding tracks, transmissions, and other tank *minutiae* but the dominant thinking of the time remained that tanks were Great War aberrations with few applications in any future conflict. The horse remained supreme.

But not everywhere. While tank development might have been neglected in the UK and France, some commercial development did take place (especially by Vickers of the UK, which exported its products widely), and active development took place in Germany and the Soviet Union.

One important development, already in being as early as 1917 (with the French Renault FT-17 light tank), was the

**Above:** An early Russian KS light infantry tank with a short-barreled 37mm gun.

universal adoption of traversing turrets in which to mount the main armament.

Limited traverse, side-mounted armament installations, as used on all of the UK's Great War tanks, were soon set aside in favor of fully-traversing turrets on the few inter-war new designs that did appear. One further detectable tendency was that much inter-war development concentrated on mobility, with protection and firepower being somewhat neglected.

That was not the only unfortunate inter-war design trend. Many inter-war designs reverted to the First World War "landship" infantry support approach, to the extent that they sprouted multiple ancillary turrets and other weapon stations that were cramped and difficult to command. Flat-sided, riveted construction tended to predominate, especially with the diminutive tankettes.

Tankettes, with a crew of one or two, seemed to offer a relatively inexpensive and simple-to-manufacture path,

Left: BT-7 tanks of the Soviet Army rumble down Gorky Street in Moscow on their way to the front line on November 7, 1941, during the Second World War.

Another development that would have unhappy results was the .one-man turret. Once again, the attractions of personnel and manufacturing economies overlooked the fact that the usual turret occupant was the tank commander. That commander had to serve the main armament, as well as commanding the tank, operating a radio, and generally observing and reacting to the tactical scene. Each task demanded the dedicated attentions of at least one crew member, so a single individual could not deal with them all out at the same time. Combat efficiency therefore suffered, as was apparent with the French tanks of 1940.

## Innovations

although time was to show they were an unfortunate blind alley. They almost completely lacked firepower and protection. Yet a great deal of inter-war development was directed towards such vehicles. At that time, many countries in Europe had extensive overseas interests, where tankettes and armored cars were well suited to maintaining law and order.

Germany and the Soviet Union, the two nations that did spend time developing the tank during the inter-war years, did not at first do so on any great scale. During the 1920s, German military activities remained restricted by the terms of the 1919 Treaty of Versailles, while the Soviet Union took time to recover from the 1917 Revolution and the subsequent Civil War. While tank hardware may have been little in evidence during the 1920s, by the 1930s both Germany and the Soviet Union were actively investigating the future form of the tank. Just as important, both were investigating how to use them to best advantage in battle.

The decision of the Soviet Union was to remain a constant until relatively recently. Tanks were to be used *en masse* as battering rams to force a way through enemy positions and overcome any opposition. The authoritarian command structure and sheer size of the Soviet armed forces of the day argued against any degree of finesse or subtlety. Soviet industry built up the ability to manufacture tanks by the thousand—not

**Above:** A PzKpfw III, with additional armor to the hull front and mantlet, in the heat of battle. This PzKpfw III has a short-barreled 7.5cm L/24 gun.

only to equip the Soviet tank formations but also to make up for the inevitable losses that their brutal ram tactics would incur.

Within Germany, a more sophisticated approach was undertaken. Despite the usual apathy from conservative military decision-makers, some staff officers managed to investigate the forms their future tanks would assume and gradually worked out novel ways to employ them. They already had the *Sturmtruppen* tactics of early 1918 with which to work. Using these tactics, well-trained, motivated, and suitably equipped infantry units had concentrated their attacks against well-reconnoitered points,

**Above:** Ace German tank commander, General Heinz Guderian, who fought throughout the Second World War.

infiltrated through them, and then spread out to create mayhem in rear areas. Resistance and strongpoints were left for follow-up formations to deal with, the

accent being on speed and mobile firepower.

*Sturmtruppen* tactics had worked well, but were dependent on the limited mobility and endurance of foot soldiers. The introduction of the tank could overcome these mobility problems, so for the German planners tanks—known to them as *Panzers*—took the place of *Sturmtruppen*. The concept coincided with the political and social changes taking place within Germany during the early 1930s and soon attracted the attentions of the new Nazi regime.

When *Panzers* were combined with swift artillery strikes, mechanized infantry, close support aircraft, and bombers, the impact of any attack they attempted could be greatly multiplied. *Blitzkrieg* (Lightning War) was born, and when deployed against

Poland and France in 1939 and 1940, the effects on the opposition were devastating, overwhelming, and rapid.

Poland and France both fell within weeks. In the process, tanks proved they could be battle winners in their own right. The battle tanks had arrived, their only apparent adversary being other tanks. Infantry support and other functions still remained, but the main functions of the tank became deep and rapid penetration, infiltration, and the disruption of the enemy's ability to conduct retaliatory operations.

As well as tactics, the German Army also developed suitable tanks to meet their requirements. Initially, German tanks, combined with their tactical deployment, managed to remain more mobile, better armored, and better armed than anything that could be fielded against them. German tank designs became accepted as the

**Left:** An early model PzKpfw IV with the short (24-caliber) 75mm gun, making it capable only of having a supporting role in battle. The German commander's uniform of black coverall and black beret dates him from the pre-war Panzertruppen.

**Right:** US infantry on patrol in August 1944 in the French town of Pontfaroy pass a damaged late model PzKpfw IV.

yardsticks to which Allied designers had to respond. These conditions applied only for the first two years of the war.

After 1941, Allied tank quantity gradually managed to overcome German quality, especially after the Germans invaded the Soviet Union in mid-1941. *Blitzkrieg* tactics were gradually limited and finally overcome by a combination of better armed and armored Allied tanks, improved anti-tank defensive measures, and the growing ability of Allied commanders to deploy their tank formations more effectively.

**Above:** A PzKpfw V Panther and a Panzer grenadier machine-gun crew in action on the Russian steppes during the Second World War.

After 1941, the imbalance between the ability of the Allies to produce more tanks than Germany became more and more pronounced. German tank designers managed to maintain an overall supremacy in tank design and armament right until the end. Unfortunately for them, they placed too much reliance on engineering flair and technology, and not enough on mass production requirements, all of which limited still further the ability of the German industrial infrastructure to manufacture tanks in the ever-growing quantities demanded.

In contrast, American industry managed to churn out 88,410 tanks by 1945, after starting from a virtually zero

**Below:** Engineers of the British Eighth Army investigate German anti-tank mines, lifted to clear the way forward in the Second World War Desert campaign. As mines became more lethal, so tanks increased their armor protection with the help of technology.

**Above:** Two British infantrymen accept the surrender of the crew of a PzKpfw III. Note the extra fuel carriers to extend the tank's range.

basis in 1941. Soviet industry also managed to produce tanks, including the superlative T-34 series, by the thousand. One Soviet tank factory was at one time producing one T-34 tank every 30 minutes. The outcome in 1945 was thus a victory of industrial capability as much as victory on the battlefield.

**Left, and right:** The fully amphibious Sherman DD (duplex drive), with its screen fully erected and showing its propellers at the rear (right), and back on dry land, with the screen in the process of collapsing (left).

## Diversification

Also apparent by 1945 was that, in armored warfare terms, the tank was no longer alone. Some of the forms that armored vehicles would assume were signaled by developments already in progress as early as 1918, although the inter-war lull in armored vehicle technology had done away with them almost entirely.

By 1945 the tank had been joined by armored personnel carriers, combat supply carriers, self--propelled artillery, combat engineer vehicles, armored bridge-layers, armored command posts, specialized reconnaissance vehicles, armored recovery vehicles, air defense vehicles, tank destroyers (a lightly armored but well-armed off-shoot of the tank that did not prosper), armored ambulances, flamethrowers, mineclearers, and so on.

Also by 1945 there was one category of tank that, while still in widespread service, was on the way out. This was the heavy tank, a vehicle that came to dominate a section of tank philosophy but which proved to be less than successful. The general intention was to produce a "breakthrough" tank with heavy protection and powerful armament that would be able to force its way unharmed through any enemy defenses. The prototype of this genre was the German *K-Wagen* of 1918 which, if it had been completed as intended, would have weighed 150 tons (152,400kg), with an armament of four 77mm guns. The end of the First World War did away with that venture, only for an updated and far less large and heavy approach to appear in 1942 with the German *Tiger tank*.

**Above:** A British Churchill tank undergoes maintenance during the Italian campaign in the Second World War. Note the adjustment to the tension of the tracks.

When it first appeared, the 88mm main gun and 100mm thick armor of the *Tiger* gave the Allies much to think about as they did not have any equivalent tank to act as a counter. Yet even the *Tiger* could be overcome by sheer weight of numbers and more powerful anti-tank guns, so it gradually lost its combat edge. The same happened with the even more powerful *Königstiger*, on which the main armament was an enhanced 88mm gun and the armor was up to 180mm thick. Even this powerful vehicle was overtaken in weight terms by the impractical *Maus*, where the combat weight would have been 188 tons (191,000 kg).

The term impractical is apposite when applied to the *Maus*, as the heavy tank had by then drastically disturbed the established firepower, protection, and mobility triumvirate by placing too much reliance on protection and firepower—and especially protection, the main cause of much of the extra weight. Even the less ambitious *Tiger* was a slow, ponderous, and unwieldy beast, while its heavier counterparts were far worse in

**Right:** During the attack on the German village of Wernberg, April 22, 1945, US infantrymen run past an M4 Sherman tank.

such respects. Their weight, coupled with being under-powered, limited their battlefield maneuverability, and also practical maneuverability, with such mundane considerations as bridge-crossing and railway truck capacities, and similar weight-imposed restrictions. In addition, heavy tanks demanded far more manufacturing and raw material resources than their lighter but more practical counterparts.

The Allies did have their heavy tanks, such as the Soviet IS-2 and IS-3, but they faded away after 1945. Others, such as the American T95 and the British

This German PzKpfw IV Ausf H has extra armor plates.

**Far left:** The famous anti-tank gun of the Second World War was the German 88mm/Flak 41—known as "the 88"—which was built as an anti-aircraft gun, seen here in the North African desert in April 1941.

**Above:** These tank barriers were known as "dragon's teeth" and were produced in great numbers in German in 1944–45 to try and thwart the Allied advance.

Tortoise, never even saw service. Other heavy tanks have appeared since 1945, typically the British Conqueror, Russian T-10, and US M103, but none have been rated as successful combat vehicles.

## Changes

The years 1939 to 1945 witnessed a quantum leap in tank design and technology, to say nothing of their tactical employment. From relatively simple and basic conditions, the tank had rapidly grown into a powerful war machine capable of transforming any combat scenario. Tanks of the 1945 period, including the US M26, the British Comet, and the German *Panther*, had virtually nothing in common with their 1939 counterparts other than the continued use of tracks on which to travel. Everything from armament to engines and drive trains had been transformed almost out of recognition.

So had methods of countering the tank. In 1939, the only viable methods of confining the activities of tanks were limited to heavy artillery, relatively puny anti-tank guns, and combat engineering measures such as anti-tank ditches. Well before the war ended, these measures

**Above:** A laser-guided projectile impacts on a tank. This Copperhead cannon-launched round is fired from a 155mm artillery tube, designed for a first-round hit.

had been joined by many others, including low-flying strike aircraft and specialized infantry tank-killer squads, but the most effective and far-reaching in combat terms were the shoulder-launched anti-tank projectile and the guided missile.

Using a simple and inexpensive rocket-launcher, such as the US M1 Bazooka, or a recoilless gun/launcher tube, such as the German *Panzerfaust*, every foot soldier gained the ability to knock out even the heaviest enemy tank, albeit only at short ranges.

These short-range weapons relied on another Second World War innovation, the shaped charge. This used chemical techniques to create an explosive-derived high temperature jet that could burn its way through armor, as

**Right:** This shoulder-launched rocket system is the British LAW-80 (Light Anti-armor Weapon), which was fielded in the 1980s—an effective line of defense against tanks.

opposed to the usual kinetic energy approach combining projectile mass and velocity to punch through armored protection.

The introduction of shoulder-launched anti-tank systems resulted in a considerable change in the age-old conflict between attack and defence, to the general detriment of the tank. They also greatly modified tank warfare techniques. It had been discovered that causing shaped charges to detonate some distance away from the target armor considerably reduced its armor penetration performance. Following a period when expedient measures were introduced, such as piling sand bags or lengths of spare tank track all around the vehicle to be protected, it was discovered that stand-off screens of light metal sheets or metal mesh panels could considerably reduce the anti-armor effects of shoulder-launched shaped charges. In addition to these defensive measures, tank commanders became reluctant to venture into localities, such as built-up areas, where such weapons were most likely to be encountered. By 1945,

**Above:** A US Marine Corps M67A2 flamethrower tank attacks Viet Cong positions in South Vietnam, 1966.

tank operations in such hazardous areas were almost always supported by infantry dedicated to keeping enemy tank-killer squads and their shaped charge launchers at a safe distance, a complete reversal of the tank's original infantry support function.

The anti-tank guided missile was also an established fact by the time the war ended in 1945. During that year the Germans began to introduce significant numbers of the X-7 *Rottkäppen* wire-controlled rocket for combat trials on the Eastern Front. From the success of those trials stemmed the huge numbers and myriad types of anti-tank guided missile now in service. Following a full-time but gradual development path that seems to be constantly introducing enhanced performance revisions, they have diversified from line-of-sight guidance into long-range systems now capable of being launched on a fire-and-forget basis to ranges measured in miles rather than yards. Free-launch system missiles can now seek out and home onto their tank targets completely under autonomous control, all without human intervention other than the launching phase. Guided missile systems have also resulted in the re-emergence of the tank destroyer, with relatively small and light armored vehicles, such as personnel carriers, being able to carry and launch long-range anti-tank missiles capable of knocking out any tank likely to be encountered.

As yet, active measures against anti-tank missiles have been relatively few. One has been the introduction of explosive reactive armor, where shaped charge jets from any weapon source can have their effects considerably reduced by explosive blocks covering the main armor detonating under the influence of the impact and disrupting the high temperature jet.

Another measure has been some form of passive radar monitoring system set around a tank turret to sense an

**Below:** The US Army's TOW (Tube-launched, Optically-guided, Wire-controlled) infantry-manned anti-tank system has a caliber of 120mm.

**Right:** The PT-76 light tank chassis is used for other applications, such as a launcher/transporter for the Frog 3 surface-to-surface missile system.

**Above:** The production line for British Chieftain tank turrets at the Royal Ordnance Factory in Leeds, northern England in the mid-1970s. The gun on the nearest turret has yet to have its thermal cladding applied.

incoming missile and launch a high explosive fragmenting package towards it to at least degrade its subsequent performance. On a more passive scale, various forms of composite armors—consisting of materials as diverse as ceramics to layers of light alloys sandwiched between other materials—can provide a far greater measure of protection than steel against all manner of kinetic and chemical energy attack. Other sensors can now add to vehicle protection by sounding alarms at the approach of a missile, or when the beam of a hostile laser rangefinder or target designator is detected. Highly efficient automatic fire suppression systems are now standard. In the last resort, the agility, speed, and maneuverability of even the largest MBTs in service can still do much to make most guided missile engagements problematic for missile system operators.

Technological advances have also provided short-range, shoulder-launched weapons with a high degree of

accuracy and kill rate, thanks to computer-controlled projectile trajectory assessment measures, to the extent that the tank is now highly vulnerable to anti-armor missiles of almost every variety.

Yet in tank versus tank engagements, the most widely used weapon remains the high velocity gun. Towed anti-tank guns have now all but faded into history but the tank gun, together with its array of advanced ammunition, remains a potent and highly effective weapon, and is expected to remain so for many years to come.

## Post 1945

The end of the war in 1945 once again further halted tank development to a considerable degree, although never to the levels plumbed after 1918. Although Germany (and Japan and Italy, both nations that contributed little of significance regarding tank development) had been defeated, a new confrontation emerged in the shape of the Cold War between the East and West power blocs. Both sides of the Cold War still had much to do to recover from 1939–45, but once confrontation became an established fact, tank developments were once again in the pipeline.

One almost universally applied development was that petrol engines were gradually replaced by diesels, usually arranged in lighter, more compact powerpacks that made power unit repairs and replacements much easier and faster than before. This development, already well established before 1945, not only introduced the safety of less flammable diesel fuel, but the increased fuel economy that could result in longer operational ranges. Engine packs also became more powerful to meet the demands for more agile performances, combined with the inevitable gradual weight increases seemingly inherent in tank development. Gas turbines seemed, for a time, to be the way ahead for tank propulsion, although the most recent developments have reverted to the more conventional diesels, which are today more compact and with much greater power than previous generations.

Tank armament has also grown in power. Tank guns have gradually grown in caliber from the modest post-war 85 or 90mm up to 120 or 125mm. Any further increases in gun size are now unlikely to occur, for as gun calibers increase, so does the bulk of the ammunition, and its stowage volume. Although 140mm guns were once considered as the next step upwards, they did not appear, other than as prototypes. The main shortcoming that emerged was that the number of operational 140mm rounds any tank can carry remains far too low for tactical and logistic comfort.

Instead, the recent accent has been on ammunition performance enhancements, especially in the field of armor-piercing, fin-stabilized, discarding-sabot (APFSDS), kinetic energy projectiles. APFSDS 120 or 125mm projectiles can now knock out almost any armored vehicle likely to be encountered at ranges of well over 9,850ft. As far as most tank gunners are concerned, the shaped charge has fallen from favor. To

**Right:** The US Army's M1 Abrams set the international standard for tank design in the 1990s and leading into the first decade of the 21st century.

**Left:** US Army 105mm APDS (Armor-Piercing Discarding Sabot) rounds are displayed before loading the tanks during Exercise Bright Star, a training exercise in the Egyptian desert in 1987.

are too prone to the influences of diverse environmental factors, including side winds, to maintain the degree of accuracy now expected. Tank guns can also launch guided projectiles with the latest versions of the Russian T-90, for example, launching a laser guided projectile out to a range of 16,400ft, beyond that of a conventional tank gun.

All the above factors apply mainly to what is now known as the main battle tank (MBT). While enormous numbers of MBTs continue to populate the tank parks of almost every armor-owning nation, the fact remains that they are now increasingly unlikely to be

create their best on-target effects, shaped charge warheads (also known as High Explosive, Anti-Tank or HEAT) have to be delivered at relatively low velocities. At all but the shortest ranges, shaped charge projectiles

employed in future combat on any significant scale, in Europe at least.

The end of the Cold War did away with the need for European nations to field the masses of complex and expensive MBTs once considered so highly necessary. Their anticipated adversary, the former Soviet Union, is no more. Tank versus tank battles are no longer envisaged, other than in a few global hot spots, such as the Near or Middle East, and the Indian sub-continent. Recent MBT development has been reduced to refinements such as improved ammunition, fire control systems, and enhanced survivability features.

The introduction of electronics has resulted in a whole host of new tank capabilities, quite apart from the ever-more complex main armament fire control systems. They include land navigation and battlefield information systems, all occupying a fraction of the space once occupied by a single radio installation. To these can be added night vision devices that allow combat to be realistically conducted under the worst possible night conditions. One result of all these new capabilities is that the tank and its associated combat vehicles are no longer just war machines: they have become weapon systems. Indeed, into today's MBTs, electronics can make up some 50 per cent of the total cost of the vehicle.

No brand new MBT designs were in prospect at the time of writing, as nearly all considerations were being directed towards keeping those already held in service for that much longer. Yet the MBT will be with us for a long while yet.

## Lighter

Another reason for the apparent demise of the MBT is that the accent these days is now on strategic rapid deployment forces delivering almost instant reactions to any source of trouble. Moving any MBT over anything other than the shortest distance involves logistics on a grand scale. Few transport aircraft can carry an MBT. What are required now are relatively light armored vehicles in all their many forms, yet with the combat power and capability once associated with MBTs.

The accent is therefore now on mobility, with wheeled vehicles once again coming into fashion. Vehicles such as the US Stryker series are much lighter than MBTs

(although only slightly less bulky), yet in some instances their main armament and electronic suites are only marginally less powerful than those of an MBT. To employ the Stryker example once again, one member of the series is armed with a high performance 105mm gun, not far removed in armor penetration terms than a first-generation 120mm MBT main gun. Guided missiles can also be carried and launched. Stryker mobility compared with an MBT is not quite in the same all-terrain class as a tracked MBT—and neither is the protection factor—but overall there remains a balance that will make the Stryker and its kind effective under all but the most extreme conditions. Fortunately for the Stryker, such conditions are foreseen as few and far between.

The Stryker is but one armored vehicle series among many, but it does provide yet another example of another armored vehicle design trend, that of "families." The intention is that one basic vehicle hull, chassis, suspension, and powerpack installation is adapted to

**Left:** A British Army FV101 Scorpion tank crosses a bridge, laid by the Royal Engineers. Scorpions were powered by the same engine as the Jaguar XK-120.

fulfil whatever combat roles are considered necessary. The Stryker was originally a Swiss MOWAG armored personnel carrier, but it has also emerged as a command vehicle, gun carrier, supply carrier, and so on—all vehicles retaining sub-system and component commonality, and all the many other maintenance and re-supply advantages that can follow. A further extension of this design versatility can still result in novel forms of "family" vehicle adding to the number of combat vehicles types. One recent example has been the NBC (Nuclear, Biological, and Chemical) reconnaissance vehicle.

Further new and lighter armored vehicles to meet the ever-changing requirements of modern warfare will no doubt emerge with time, although it has to be re-emphasized that the MBT remains a powerful combat vehicle that will remain viable for many combat roles for a good time to come. While the US and some European countries are working on new armored vehicles suitable for worldwide deployment by air, other countries are still maintaining their MBT fleets—this especially applies to countries in the Middle East, as well as China, India, and Pakistan.

# 1

# ARGENTINA, AUSTRIA, BRAZIL, CANADA, CHINA, CROATIA, CZECH REPUBLIC

**Left:** The most advanced armored vehicle ever built in Brazil was this ENGESA EE-T1 Osorio Main Battle Tank.

**Above:** The TAM tank was designed in Germany and then manufactured in Argentina by TAMSE. Main armament is a stabilized 105mm gun with a 7.62mm co-axial machine gun, and a similar weapon on the turret roof for air defense.

**Right:** As well as the TAM tank, TAMSE developed a family of vehicles on the same chassis, including an infantry fighting vehicle, command post vehicle, 120mm mortar carrier, surface to surface rocket launcher, and 155mm self-propelled gun.

**Above:** The SK 105 was originally developed to meet the requirements of the Austrian Army for a highly mobile tank destroyer, and was subsequently built in large numbers for the home and export markets.

**Right: The** main armament of the SK 105 is a 105mm rifled gun in an oscillating turret, with the last versions fitted with an advanced fire control system and day/night sights.

**Left:** Brazilian firm Bernardini developed a complete family of light tanks and variants for the Brazilian Army in the 1970s, including this X1A2 light tank armed with a 90mm gun.

**Below:** Line-up of Bernardini X1A light tanks awaiting delivery to the Brazilian Army.

**Left:** As a private venture, Brazilian firm ENGESA developed the EE-T1 Osorio Main Battle Tank and prototypes were built armed with 105mm and 120mm guns coupled to an advanced computerized fire control system. It had many other advanced features but never went into production. ENGESA no longer exists.

**Above:** A Bernardini X1A2 is put through its paces. This was an evolutionary development of the earlier X1A and X1A1 light tanks developed by the company in the late 1970s.

**Right:** Main armament of the Bernardini X1A2 was a 90mm gun that was also installed in the Brazilian ENGESA EE-9 (6x6). Cascavel armored guns were used heavily by the Brazilian Army.

**Below:** The Sexton self-propelled gun was developed to meet the requirements of the British Army and based on a RAM tank chassis. It was armed with a 25-pounder field gun with limited traverse. Some 2,150 were built in Canada between 1943 and 1945, and continued in service with a number of countries such as India and South Africa well after the Second World War.

**Right:** The RAM I tank was developed in Canada with the first prototypes completed mid-1941, followed by 50 production vehicles. Production then switched to the more advanced RAM II, shown here armed with a 6-pounder gun. Production of the RAM II continued until 1943, by which time 1,899 had been built. These were used for training in Canada and the UK, but these units were re-equipped with Sherman tanks before the D-Day landings in June 1944. Many RAM II had their turrets removed and converted into Kangaroo armored personnel carriers.

In the 1950s, Russia supplied China with a quantity of T-54 tanks. Subsequently manufactured in China as the Type 59, large numbers were built for the home and export market. They were all armed with the standard 100mm rifled gun, with later production vehicles featuring gun stabilization systems and infra-red night vision equipment. Further development resulted in the Type 69 tank. This had a number of improvements, with the Type 69-I having a smooth bore gun and the Type 69-II a rifled gun.

**Below:** Another variant based on the Type 69 chassis was this twin 37mm self-propelled air defense system, fitted with a surveillance radar on the turret roof, which was retracted when traveling.

**Above:** One of many versions of the Type 69 MBT is this Type 84 armored vehicle launched bridge, here launching its bridge over the vehicle front.

## SPECIFICATIONS

| | |
|---|---|
| Nationality | China |
| Armor | 30–100mm |

| | |
|---|---|
| Length/width | 29ft 6in / 10ft 9in |
| Number built | not known |
| 1st prototype run | early 1950s |

**Below:** People's Liberation Army infantry move forward to support Type 59 tanks. This was essentially the Russian T-54 and formed the basis of Chinese tanks for many years. It was followed by the Type 69, Type 79, and Type 80.

**Left:** Chinese Type 69-II tank armed with 100mm gun and laser rangefinder mounted on mantlet to improve first round hit probability. This vehicle also has an infra-red search light mounted co-axial with the main armament.

**Below:** Chinese Type 69 series command tank which has additional communications equipment for its specialized role.

**Left:** To support the Type 69 tank, China developed the Type 653 armored recovery vehicle. To carry out its specialized role, this has a front-mounted dozer/stabilizer blade, winches, and a crane with a telescopic jib that can lift complete powerpacks. Large numbers of Type 653s have been built for the home and export markets. This particular vehicle was used by the Iraqi Army.

**Left:** The Chinese Type 80 tank has a 105mm rifled gun coupled to a computerized day/night fire control system with the laser rangefinder being mounted externally over the main armament. This model has long-range fuel tanks at the rear.

**Above:** Type 80 tank from the rear without long-range fuel tanks fitted. The wire basket around the turret rear is used to stow the crew equipment, as well as providing some protection against high explosive anti-tank projectiles.

**Below:** Pakistan has taken delivery of large numbers of these Chinese Type 85-IIAP tanks, armed with a 125mm smooth bore gun which is fed by an automatic loader that allowed the crew to be reduced to three people.

**Above:** Type 85 series tanks in quantity production for the People's Liberation Army. This tank has a much higher level of armor protection than earlier Chinese tanks, especially over the vital frontal arc.

**Left:** The Type 85 tank has also been produced in Pakistan under a co-production plan and has been constantly improved since it first entered service some years ago. Standard equipment includes a computerized day/night fire control system.

**Right:** The latest tank to enter service with the People's Liberation Army is the Type 98, which has the 125mm smooth bore gun fed by an automatic loader. It also has a high level of protection and a roof mounted laser dazzle device.

SĐ5/TRUNG-ĐOÀN 7 BB TỊCH THU TẠI AN-LỘC

**Left:** Chinese Type 63 light amphibious tank knocked out in South Vietnam. This vehicle saw considerable combat service in South Vietnam, where its small size and light weight proved highly effective in the hands of a well-trained crew. Its thin armor could be penetrated by heavy machine gun fire and anti-tank teams equipped with rocket launchers firing high explosive anti-tank (HEAT) warheads. It was operated by a crew of four comprising commander, gunner, loader, and driver.

**Right:** The Type 63 light tank is fully amphibious, propelled in the water by two waterjets situated either side at the rear of the hull. Before entering the water a trim vane is erected at the front of the hull and the bilge pumps switched on. In People's Liberation Army service the vehicles are being upgraded to include a turret armed with a 105mm gun coupled to a computerized fire control system. This is designated the Type 63A.

**Left:** The Degman Main Battle Tank has been developed in Croatia and is a further progression of the late production M-84 series vehicle. It features a new all-welded steel turret which is easier to produce than a conventional cast turret.

**Above:** To provide higher battlefield survivability, the Croatian Degman MBT is fitted over the frontal arc with panels of explosive reactive armor. This provides additional protection against anti-tank weapons and missiles with HEAT warheads.

**Below:** The Czech LT vz 38 tank's main armament was a 37mm gun with a 7.92mm machine gun mounted co-axial and similar weapons in the hull. First vehicles were completed in May 1939 and taken over by the German Army as the PzKpfw 38 (t). The tank on the right is a PzKpfw III.

**Right:** The German Army used significant quantities of the Czech LT-38 tank under the designation PzKpfw 38 (t). These were used by the 7th and 8th Panzer Division during the invasion of France in 1940, and remained in front-line service for several years. When it became obsolete as a tank, many of these chassis were converted for more specialized roles.

**Above: A** German PzKpfw 38 (t) tank and motorcycle combination in November 1940. The speed and agility of the Czech designed-and-built tank made it ideal for the tactics of the German Army. Production of the vehicle continued in occupied Czechoslovakia for some years, and production ultimately reached a total of 1,414 units.

**Below:** Prior to being accepted for service with the Czech Republic, the upgraded T-72CZ M4 underwent extensive cold weather trials.

**Above:** Prototype of the upgraded Czech Republic T-72CZM4 during fording trials, showing the additional explosive reactive armor installed over the frontal arc for higher protection. The first of these upgraded vehicles were delivered to the Czech Republic in 2003.

**Right:** In addition to the new armor package, the Czech Republic upgraded T-72CZM4 has other improvements, including a new computerized fire control system from Italy, and a new powerpack from Israel, which features a Perkins V-12 diesel engine and an Allison automatic transmission.

# 2

# FRANCE, GERMANY

**Left:** The French Schneider assault tank first saw action in April 1917, with 400 built by the end of the First World War. The tank had a crew of six, and was armed with a single 75mm howitzer, positioned in the right side of the hull, and two 8mm machine guns. The latter were mounted one each side of the hull. Later in the war some were fitted with additional armor, while others were converted into supply carriers.

**Above:** The Char 2C heavy tank was developed towards the end of the First World War, but never saw combat. A total of ten were built and these were still in service with the French Army at the outbreak of the Second World War. The turret was armed with a 75mm gun, with an 8mm machine gun mounted in a turret at the rear with additional machine guns in the front, and one on either side firing forwards.

**Below:** Large numbers of captured Renault FT-17 light tanks and a single Char B1 gathered together at a Wehrmacht depot in Poland in 1941. These were then converted to a number of specialized roles, because as a light tank they were obsolete. Some FT-17s were used to guard airfields and other strategic areas, while their turrets were removed and used in fixed fortifications.

**Above:** A somewhat jaded FT-17 light tank without its 8mm machine gun, showing the suspension and track with its large front driving sprocket. The Renault four cylinder water cooled petrol engine was located at the rear.

**Right:** After the fall of France in 1940 many Renault FT-17 light tanks were refurbished and taken into service with the German Army as the PzKpfw 18R 730 (f), although by this time they were clearly obsolete and had only limited military use.

**Above:** Renault FT-17 light tank of the French Army returns from an operation on the Aisne front in 1940. The vehicle is fully closed down, with the commander inside the turret, rather than sitting on top of the vehicle.

**Right:** The Renault FT-17 light tank also saw combat use after the fall of France in 1940, such as in North Africa. A column of Indian Army Bren gun carriers moves through a demolished road block consisting of a PzKpfw 18R 730(f) ex-French Army light tank, and an ex-French Army anti-tank gun.

**Above:** Renault FT-17 light tanks were also supplied to the US Army towards the end of the First World War. This FT-17 is fitted with an additional fuel tank at the rear to extend its operational range. (Photograph taken in September 1918.)

**Left:** French-built Renault FT-17 light tanks operated by the US Army's 326th Tank Battalion move up towards the frontline near Boureuilles in September 1918.

**Right:** The Renault RT-17 had a crew of two—driver and commander. The driver sat at the front and viewed the terrain through two small, un-protected vision slits.

**Below:** Following the end of the First World War, the French Army moved into Germany and these FT-17 light tanks are on the steets of Frankfurt watched by apprehensive German civilians.

**Left:** The French St Chamond assault tank was based on a lengthened Holt tractor chassis, with a hull of riveted armored steel, and had a crew of eight. Armed with a 75mm gun and four 8mm machine guns, it first saw action in May 1917, when 15 of the 16 vehicles became stuck in the first line of defense.

**Above:** The French Army took delivery of ten of these Char 2C heavy tanks at the end of the First World War, but they never saw any combat. Still in service with the French Army in 1940, they were knocked out while being transported on their special railway wagons by the Luftwaffe in 1940.

**Above:** The Renault AMC 35 light tank was developed as a follow-on to the Renault FT-17 fielded during the First World War. Production began in 1935, and over 900 had been built by the time of the German invasion in 1940. The vehicle had a crew of two—driver and commander. The latter commanded the tank, as well as loaded and operated the main armament.

**Right:** Following the fall of France in 1940, large quantities of French Army equipment was taken into service by the German Army, including this Hotchkiss H-39 light tank which was then designated the PzKpfw 39H (f). This vehicle is fitted with a skid tail to enable it to cross trenches, and a German type vertical radio antenna.

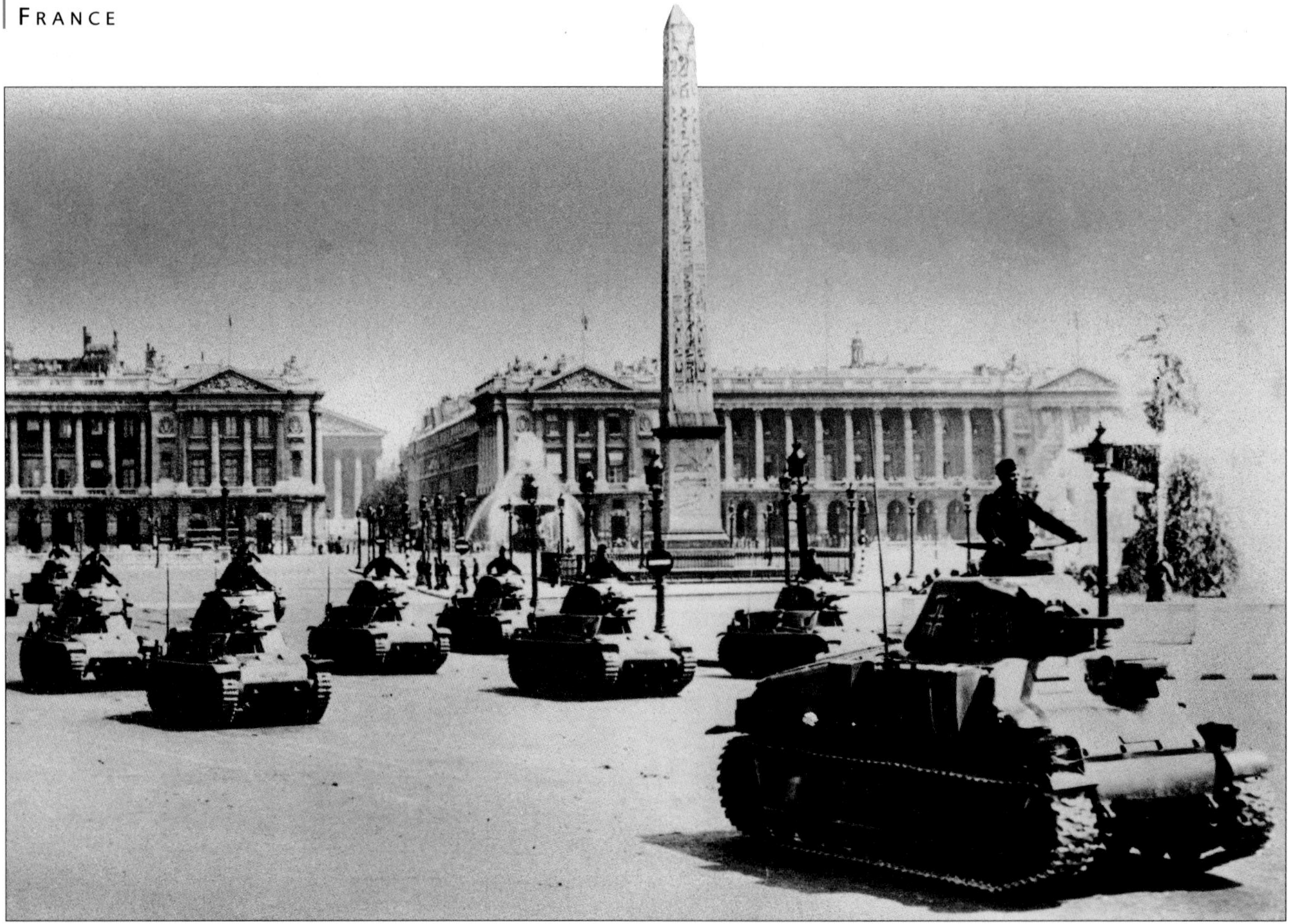

**Left:** A humiliating scene for the people of Paris, as a German tank squadron of captured French Army SOMUA S-35 medium tanks (designated PzKpfw 35C 739 [f]), and Hotchkiss H-39 light tanks (designated PzKpfw 39H [f]), parade past.

**Above:** Captured French Army Hotchkiss H-39 light tank used by the German Army as the PzKpfw 39H (f). Many were subsequently rebuilt into more specialized roles, such as 75mm self-propelled anti-tank guns.

**Above:** French Army Char B1 heavy tank abandoned in a French street during the fighting in May/June 1940. The Char B1 had a crew of four and was armed with a 75mm gun in the hull, and a turret-mounted 37mm gun, plus two 7.5mm machine guns.

**Right:** German infantry pass a French Army Char B1 series heavy tank during the fighting in France in May/June 1940. The 75mm short-barreled gun mounted in the front of the vehicle was fixed and aimed by the driver traversing the tank.

**Left:** Following the fall of France in 1940, many Char B1-bis heavy tanks were taken into service with the German Army. This one was converted into the Pz Kpfw B1 Flamm (f) configuration, with the hull-mounted 75mm gun replaced by a flamethrower. A total of 24 were modified between 1942–43. The turret, armed with a 37mm gun and machine gun, was retained. Some also had their turrets and hull armament removed, and were fitted with a 105mm howitzer.

**Left and below:** Front and top drawings of the French Char B1-bis heavy tank. Some 365 had been built by 1940. This vehicle had the fighting compartment at the front and engine compartment at the rear, with the tracks running around the sides of the hull. This was one of the most well-armed and protected of the French tanks during the Battle of France in 1940. Many were captured by the Germans and taken into service as the PzKpfw B1 (f). The latter letter indicating its country of origin, in this case France.

**Below and right:** The Renault AMR 35 light tank was a follow-on to the earlier AMR 33, and also had a hull and turret of riveted construction. This vehicle is armed with a 13.2mm Hotchkiss heavy air cooled machine gun, and had a crew of two—commander/gunner, and driver. Other versions had different armament, including a 7.5mm MG31 machine gun or even a 25mm Hotchkiss anti-tank gun. A total of 200 were built, and following the fall of France many were taken over by the German Army and used for specialized roles.

**Left:** The German Army took over many Renault R-35 light tanks. Some were converted into specialist roles—such as this self-propelled anti-tank gun fitted with a captured Czech 47mm weapon—but there were many other versions, such as ammunition carrier, 105mm howitzer, and 80mm mortar.

**Below:** The French Army took delivery of about 100 of these Renault AMC 35 light tanks, and 12 were also sold to Belgium in 1937. Main armament comprised a 47mm gun and a 7.5mm co-axial machine gun. Some were taken over by the German Army and then designated PzKpfw AMC 738 (f).

**Left and right:** Front and rear views of the French Renault R-35 tank, which had a hull and turret of cast armor construction. Playing card insignia were often painted on French Army vehicles to identify sub units. While having adequate armor and firepower, the Renault R-35 light tank was too slow.

**Above:** Knocked out Renault R-35 light tank. After the fall of France, many of these were taken into service with the German Army as a reconnaissance vehicle under the designation Pzkpfw R-35 (4.7cm). Some were also converted into more specialist roles, such as self-propelled anti-tank guns, ammunition resupply vehicles, and self-propelled howitzers.

**Right:** The German Army captured many SOMUA S-35 medium tanks and took them into service under the designation PzKpfw 35C 739 (f).

**Below:** New French SOMUA S-35 medium tank leaves the plant on a trailer towed by a half-tracked vehicle.

**Right:** The French SOMUA S-35 had a hull constructed of castings bolted together. The crew of three were the driver and radio operator, seated at the front of the vehicle, and the commander in the turret, who also had to aim, load, and fire the armament, consisting of a 47mm gun and 7.5mm machine gun.

**Left:** ARL-44 heavy tanks of the French 503rd Regiment made their only public appearance in Paris on July 14, 1951. The intention was to build some 300 ARL-44s, but only 60 were built. Main armament consisted of a 90mm gun with a 7.5mm co-axial machine gun, and provision for a similar weapon mounted on the turret roof for air defense purposes.

**Below:** In the late 1930s, the ARL (Atelier de Construction de Rueil) started development work on a project to mount a 75mm gun in a new turret of the Char B1 heavy tank chassis. This was still on the drawing board at the time of the German occupation, but work continued in secret and after the liberation of Paris, production began under the designation ARL-44. The driver and co-driver were seated at the front, with commander, gunner, and loader in the turret. This was to have been replaced by the AMX-50, but large numbers of US-supplied M47 tanks were available and the ARL-44 was soon phased out of service.

# *Profile:* FRANCE: AMX-13

Shortly after the end of the Second World War the French Army formulated plans for a number of new armored fighting vehicles, including a new light tank. This emerged as the AMX-13—AMX being the original design authority, Atelier de Construction d'Issy-les-Moulineaux, and 13, the original design weight in tonnes. First prototypes were completed in 1947/48 and production was soon underway at the Atelier de Construction Roanne, although it later transferred to Chalon-sur-Saone. The first models were armed with a 75mm gun in an oscillating turret, but later models had a 90mm or 105mm gun.

**Right:** The AMX-13 light tank has a crew of three—driver, commander, and gunner. No loader was required, as the 75mm gun was fed by a bustle-mounted automatic loader, which consisted of two revolver type magazines which each held six rounds of ready-use ammunition. When the main armament was fired, the empty cartridge cases were ejected out of the turret bustle.

## SPECIFICATIONS

| | | | |
|---|---|---|---|
| **Nationality** | France | **Length/width** | 20ft 10in / 8ft 2in |
| **Armor** | 0.4-1.6in (10-40 mm) | **Engine** | SOFAM 8-cylinder |
| **Combat weight** | 33,070lb (15,000kg) | **Number built** | approximately 3,500 |
| | | **1st prototype run** | 1947/48 |

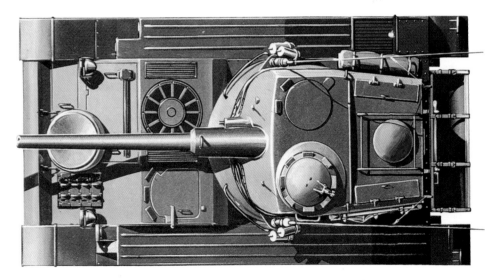

**This page:** Three-view drawing of a basic French Army AMX-13 light tank, armed with a 75mm gun. These were later up-gunned with a more effective 90mm gun.

**Above:** AMX-13 light tank up-gunned with a 90mm gun fitted with a muzzle brake, and thermal sleeve. Large numbers of AMX-13s and their variants were built, and many remain in service today, especially in South America and Asia.

**Right:** To back up the AMX-13, a complete family of specialist support vehicles were developed. This armored recovery vehicle was fitted with specialized equipment for its role, including a winch and crane.

**Below:** The light weight of the AMX-13 allows it to be rapidly transported by land, sea, and air. In the 1950s and 1960s, it saw extensive combat use—not only with the French Army in North Africa, but in other parts of the world, such as the Middle East and Asia.

**Right:** AMX-13 with its main armament fixed in the upper part of the oscillating turret, and gun in travelling lock.

**Below:** The AMX-13 chassis was used for other roles such as this armored ambulance.

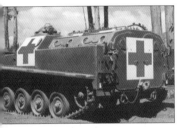

**Above:** The French AMX-13 and its variants were adopted by many countries.

**Left:** One of the more interesting French armored vehicles of the 1960s was the Hotchkiss Rive Light Fighting Unit (LFU). Developed as a private venture, it was marketed with a range of turrets, including this oscillating turret armed with a 90mm gun fed by an automatic loader and a 7.62mm machine gun.

**Above:** This version of the Light Fighting Unit is armed with two 30mm cannon and two machine guns in a one-person oscillating turret. There was also a tank destroyer version armed with two SS 12 or four SS 11 wire guided anti-tank missiles and a command post vehicle.

**Left:** In the 1980s the French company Creusot-Loire developed the MARS 15 family of light armored vehicles. This is the light tank model, fitted with a Giat Industries TS 90 turret armed with a 90mm gun, which could fire armor piercing fin stabilized discarding sabot ammunition. It was offered to a number of customers, but never entered quantity production—the company no longer exists.

**Above:** In addition to the MARS 15 light tank with the TS 90 turret (left), the MARS 15 chassis was also marketed as an infantry fighting vehicle, fitted with a turret that was armed with a 25mm cannon, but this never progressed beyond the prototype stage. To reduce costs, the MARS 15 family used proven commercial components wherever possible.

Development of the Giat Industries AMX-30 main battle tank (MBT) began in the 1950s, with the first proto- types completed in 1961. Production was well underway by 1996. Large numbers were built for the home and export markets, although in French Army service it has almost been replaced by the Giat Industries Leclerc MBT. The hull and turret was of cast armor construction. Main armament is a 105mm gun, with co-axial weapon normally a 20mm cannon or a 12.7mm machine gun. A 7.62mm machine gun is mounted at the commander's station.

**Left:** An early model of the AMX-30 MBT, with a large infra-red (IR) searchlight mounted to the left of the main armament. While an adequate vehicle, the AMX-30 was not as reliable a vehicle as the German Leopard 1 developed at the same time. The French Army upgraded the AMX-30 in a number of key areas, including replacing the IR night vision equipment by thermal devices.

**Above:** The AMX-30 chassis was used in a wide range of versions. One of the more interesting is this model, which was designed to carry and launch the Pluton surface-to-surface missile fitted with a tactical nuclear warhead. This was only used by the French Army and has now been withdrawn from service.

**Below:** The AMX-30 DCA was developed by France to meet the requirements of Saudi Arabia and is a modified AMX-30 tank chassis fitted with a power operated turret armed with two 30mm rapid fire cannon.

| SPECIFICATIONS | | | |
|---|---|---|---|
| Nationality | France | Length/width | 31ft 1in/10ft 2in |
| Armor | 0.8-3.1in (20-81mm) | Engine | HS 110 12-cylinder |
| Combat weight | 81,600lb | Number built | 2,000 plus variants |
| | | 1st prototype run | 1960 |

**Right:** This is an upgraded French Army AMX-30B2 with the old infra-red night vision equipment replaced by a thermal camera mounted co-axial with the 105mm gun. This allowed targets to be detected and engaged at much longer ranges under day and night conditions.

**Above:** Significant export sales of the AMX-30 main battle tank were made to countries including Chile, Cyprus, Qatar, Saudi Arabia, Spain, United Arab Emirates, and Venezuela. It has seen combat service in the Middle East.

**Above:** The French Army still has a small number of units equipped with the AMX-30B2 main battle tank, and to improve their battlefield survivability they have been fitted with explosive reactive armor over their frontal arc. This is designed to neutralize anti-tank weapons fitted with a high explosive anti-tank (HEAT) warhead.

**Left and below:** The AMX-32 main battle tank was developed by Giat Industries from the earlier AMX-30, and featured advanced armor over the frontal arc. It was armed with a 105mm or 120mm gun with a 20mm co-axial cannon coupled to a computerized fire control system.

**Right:** AMX-32 MBT from the rear with the commander's cupola on the right. The AMX-32 never entered quantity production, as export customers were reluctant to place orders for equipment that was not already type classified and in service with the French Army.

**Above:** The Leclerc MBT is fitted with a computerized day/night fire control system, allowing the 120mm gun, whether at rest or moving, to be laid onto the target, with a high first-round hit probability.

**Right:** Just part of a French Army Leclerc main battle tank regiment lined up together with some its support vehicles, including AMX-10P and VAB personnel carriers, and VBL scout cars.

**Left:** AMX-40 MBT was developed by Giat Industries for the export market, especially the Middle East. It was armed with a 120mm smooth bore gun.

**Above:** The AMX-40 MBT was an evolutionary development of the AMX-32. It had greater protection and improved mobility, but never entered production.

**Below:** The Leichte Kampfwagen II (LK II) cavalry tank was similar to the British Whippet tank, with the engine compartment at the front and the crew of three at the rear. Main armament was a 5.7cm gun and one or two 7.92mm Maxim machine guns. Only two vehicles were built and it never saw combat service, although the design was later sold to Sweden.

**Opposite page:** Head on view of the German Leichte Kampfwagen II (LK II), clearly showing the 5.7cm gun mounted at the rear with limited traverse, and the mounting for the 7.92mm Maxim machine gun on the opposite side.

**Above:** The German Stürmpanzerwagen A7V crew rest behind the front lines in the summer of 1918. This version was armed with six or seven 7.92mm Maxim machine guns at various points around the hull of the vehicle. A total of 100 were ordered, but only 20 were completed by the end of the war. Today, there is only one in existence in Australia.

**Right and far right:** Front and side drawings of the A7V; the left drawing shows the 5.7cm gun which had limited traverse over the frontal arc. The A7V first saw combat in March 1918 and was normally deployed in units of five vehicles. The vehicle had a crew of 18, but was unreliable. When compared to British designs, it had limited trench crossing ability.

**Above:** In the 1930s Germany built a small batch of experimental tanks called PzKpfw V, which had a crew of seven and was fitted with one turret in the centre armed with a 75mm gun and a 37mm co-axial gun. The vehicle also had two additional turrets to the front and rear of the main turret, armed with two 7.92mm MG13 machine guns. It was powered by a Maybach V-12 water-cooled inline petrol engine, developing 360hp.

**Right:** The German PzKpfw V experimental tank was typical of a number of other tanks developed in the 1920s and 1930s, and never entered quantity production. A total of six vehicles were built of which only one was armored. These never saw combat, although at least four went to Norway where they were photographed on a jetty, and for some years it was believed that the vehicle had entered quantity production. This was not the case.

**Left:** Rare photograph of the Infanterie-begleitpanzer version in 1939.

**Below:** German PzKpfw I tanks during a training exercise in 1941. This was only meant to be an interim design, but well over 2,000 were built.

**Right:** Following its withdrawal from front-line service, many German PzKfpw I tanks were converted into specialized roles such as this Panzerjager (tank hunter). Seen here in a French village in 1940, it was fitted with a turret armed with a 4.7cm Pak anti-tank gun.

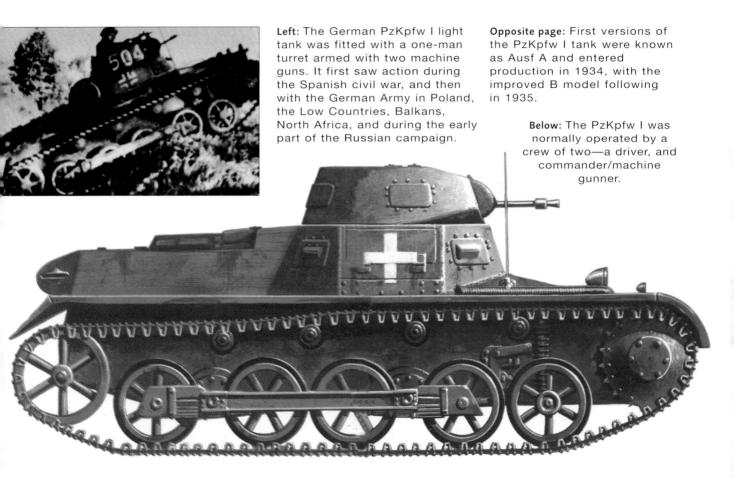

**Left:** The German PzKpfw I light tank was fitted with a one-man turret armed with two machine guns. It first saw action during the Spanish civil war, and then with the German Army in Poland, the Low Countries, Balkans, North Africa, and during the early part of the Russian campaign.

**Opposite page:** First versions of the PzKpfw I tank were known as Ausf A and entered production in 1934, with the improved B model following in 1935.

**Below:** The PzKpfw I was normally operated by a crew of two—a driver, and commander/machine gunner.

**Left:** A PzKpfw II shows its mobility on a German Army training ground. Suspension consisted of five large road wheels on quarter elliptic leaf springs, giving a good ride.

**Below:** The German Army captured large numbers of Czechoslovakian light tanks early in the Second World War, and these were soon placed into service. Production continued under the German occupation.

**Left:** A mixed group of German Army tracked and wheeled vehicles are brought to a halt by a river during the invasion of France in 1940. In the background, German engineers in inflatable boats are already at work. Vehicles shown include two PzKpfw 35 (t) light tanks captured during the invasion of Czechoslovakia and a single PzKpfw II tank on the right.

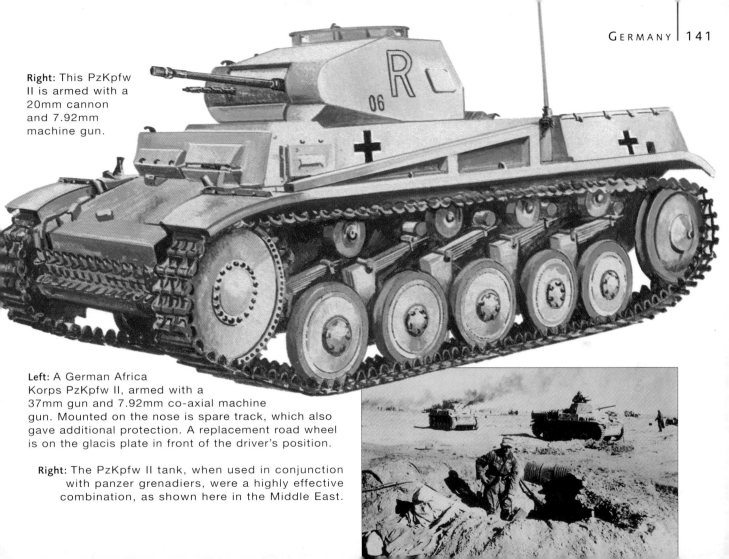

**Right:** This PzKpfw II is armed with a 20mm cannon and 7.92mm machine gun.

**Left:** A German Africa Korps PzKpfw II, armed with a 37mm gun and 7.92mm co-axial machine gun. Mounted on the nose is spare track, which also gave additional protection. A replacement road wheel is on the glacis plate in front of the driver's position.

**Right:** The PzKpfw II tank, when used in conjunction with panzer grenadiers, were a highly effective combination, as shown here in the Middle East.

The PzKpfw III tank was developed in the mid-1930s and was finally accepted for service in 1939. A total of 98 vehicles were ready by the time of the invasion of Poland, increasing to 350 when France was invaded in May 1940. Early versions had a 37mm gun, although this was soon replaced by a more effective 50mm weapon.

In addition, there was also a 7.92mm co-axial machine gun and a similar weapon was mounted in the bow of the tank next to the driver.

**Below:** A PzKpfw III tank advances during the North African campaign. It shows the additional fuel tanks to extend operational range of the vehicle. All too often, fuel tankers could not get up to the front line.

## SPECIFICATIONS

| | | | | | |
|---|---|---|---|---|---|
| **Nationality** | German | **Combat weight** | 42,770lb | **Engine** | Maybach HL 120 TRM |
| **Armor** | ·1.18–3.54in (30–90mm) | **Length/width** | 17ft 8in / 9ft 6in | **Number built** | approximately 6,000 |
| | | | | **1st prototype run** | 1935 |

The PzKpfw Aust C was armed with a long barreled 37mm L/45 gun and two 7.92mm machine guns.

**Below:** Much of the success of the German Army was due to the high level of co-operation between tanks, infantry, artillery, and aircraft.

**Right:** A PzKpfw III tank knocked out by the Russian Army on the Eastern Front. At the time of Operation Barbarossa, there were some 1,500 of these tanks in service with the German Army, but they had insufficient firepower to take on and defeat the Russian T-34 and KV series tanks. A crash program was started to improve their firepower and armor protection.

**Above:** A British Daimler scout car pauses alongside a knocked out PzKpfW III tank in the Western Desert late in 1941. The PzKpfW III proved highly effective in North Africa, and its gun out-ranged the 2-pounder gun fitted into British tanks of the period.

**Left:** Italian officials and apprehensive looking locals watch PzKpfw III of the recently formed Africa Corps through their town in 1941. Note the identification letters on the turret of the right tank and extensive external stowage.

**Below:** A German PzKpfw III tank advances into Russia in 1941. Early on in the campaign it gave a good account of itself, but was soon outclassed by the more recent Russian T-34 medium and KV series heavy tanks.

**Left:** German infantry climb aboard the rear of a German PzKpfw III tank during the advance across North Africa to Tobruk. Small arms ammunition boxes have already been loaded aboard the tank and the soldier to the left of the tank commander is carrying a flame thrower with the fuel cans strapped to his back. Due to a lack of armored personnel carriers, it was quite common for infantry to be carried forward on the back of tanks, although they were highly vulnerable to small arms fire and shell splinters.

The German PzKpfw IV medium tank was the only German tank in continuous production throughout the Second World War. Development began in 1935, with the first vehicles completed the following year, armed with a short barreled 75mm gun. It had a crew of three—commander, gunner, and loader in the electrically operated turret, with the driver and bow machine gunner in the front hull. Development of the KzKpz IV was continuous, with the Ausf D taking part in the Polish and French campaigns, supporting the PzKpfw III. As a result of combat experience additional armor was fitted, and this and other features were incorporated into the Ausf E. The next model, the Ausf F, was fitted with the highly potent 75mm KwK40 L/48 gun. The Ausf G had thicker armor, plus additional spaced armor on the turret and hull for increased protection against anti-tank weapons. The final model was the Ausf J which was simplified to speed up production.

**Left:** Head on view of the German PzKpfw IV medium tank clearly showing the additional spaced armor fitted to hull and turret for increased protection.

**Right:** German PzKpfw IV Ausf A of the 1st Panzer Division armed with a short 75mm gun and large dustbin type cupola on the turret roof. Only 35 of this model were built.

## SPECIFICATIONS

| | |
|---|---|
| Nationality | Germany |
| Armor | 0.79–3.54in (20–90mm) |
| Combat weight | 43,430lb |
| Length/width | 19ft 5in / 9ft 6in |
| Engine | Maybach HL 120 TRM |
| Number built | 8,000 plus |
| 1st prototype run | 1935 |

**Below:** An elderly Russian couple, returning home in 1944, pass a knocked out German PzKpfw IV Ausf H tank. This photograph clearly shows the long barreled 75mm gun and the 7.92mm MG 34 bow mounted machine gun. Additional armor has been fitted to the hull and turret to increase protection against anti-tank weapons.

**Above:** One of the final versions of the PzKpfw IV was this Panzerbefehlswagen mit 7.45cm KwK L/48 (armored command vehicle with 7.5cm gun, 48 caliber). This belongs to the SS Panzer Regiment 12 of the Hitlerjugend (Hitler Youth) Division.

**Right:** An early model of the PzKpfw V medium tank armed with the original short barrel 75mm gun deployed in North Africa with three of the crew of five seated outside rather than in the hot interior. The 75mm gun was soon replaced by a more potent, long barreled weapon of the same caliber.

**Left:** German PzKpfw IV medium tank armed with the long barreled 75mm gun fitted with a muzzle brake. The commander is shown here using the hatches in the turret side.

**Above:** Disabled PzKpfw IV Ausf H tanks on the Voronezh front in 1943 fitted with spaced armor designed to detonate high explosive anti-tank (HEAT) projectiles before they penetrated the main tank armor.

The Panther was developed from 1942 to counter the Russian T-34. Like the T-34, the German PzKpfw V Panther incorporated well sloped armor and was armed with a highly effective 75mm gun and two 7.92mm machine guns. It first saw combat in 1943 when numerous shortcomings became apparent, as it was rushed into production before all the faults had been rectified. By the end of the war over 3,900 Panthers had been built, although its complicated design meant that the monthly target production rate of 600 vehicles a month could never be achieved. It was considered by many to be the best tank developed in Germany during the Second World War.

## SPECIFICATIONS

| | |
|---|---|
| Nationality | Germany |
| Armor | 0.6–4.72 in (20–120mm) |
| Combat weight | 98,760lb |

**Above:** The PzKpfw V Panther was armed with a long barreled 75mm gun.

**Left:** PzKpfw V Panther with turret knocked off as a result of ammunition exploding.

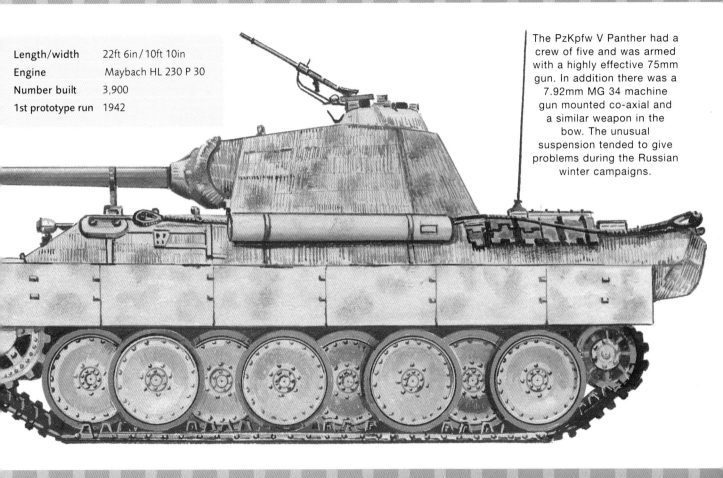

| Length/width | 22ft 6in / 10ft 10in |
|---|---|
| Engine | Maybach HL 230 P 30 |
| Number built | 3,900 |
| 1st prototype run | 1942 |

The PzKpfw V Panther had a crew of five and was armed with a highly effective 75mm gun. In addition there was a 7.92mm MG 34 machine gun mounted co-axial and a similar weapon in the bow. The unusual suspension tended to give problems during the Russian winter campaigns.

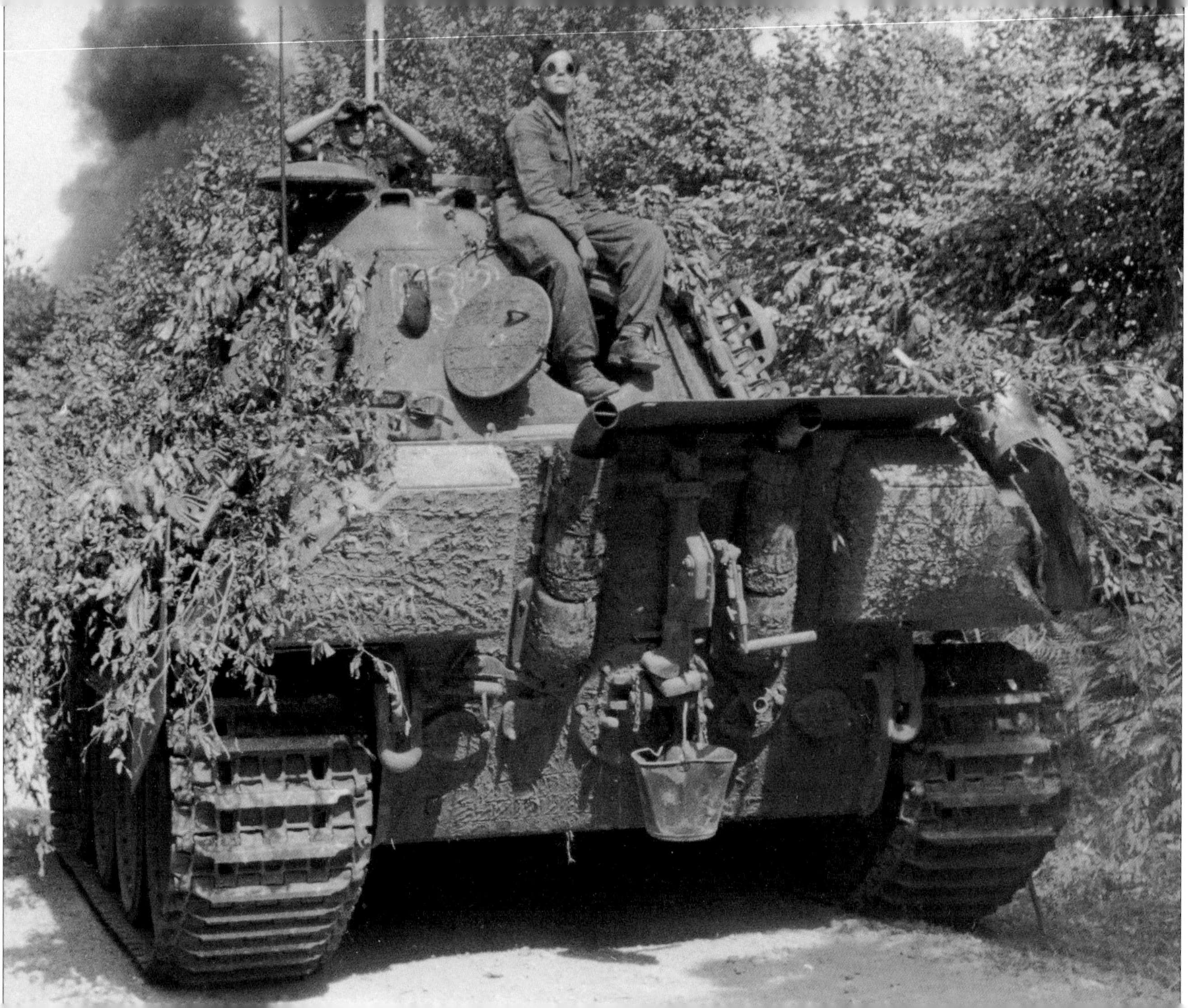

**Left:** The PzKpfw V Panther awaits action with the crew scanning the skies for allied aircraft, which were a much greater threat than enemy armor. This photograph is taken from the rear and shows the escape hatch in turret rear.

**Above:** A German PzKpfw V Panther deployed in the hull down position for maximum protection during the Italian campaign. Some Panthers were used by the French Army after the end of the Second World War.

**Above:** A radio operator of a German PzKpfw V Panther tank takes a breather. This photograph clearly shows the thick coating of Zimmerit to stop magnetic mines being attached to the tank.

**Right:** A batch of PzKpfw V Panther tanks leave the MAN facility. Target production was 600 vehicles a month, but this was never achieved, as the tank was far to complicated to build in large numbers.

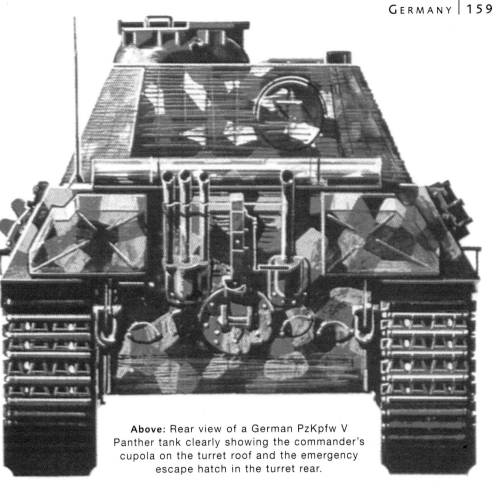

**Above:** Rear view of a German PzKpfw V Panther tank clearly showing the commander's cupola on the turret roof and the emergency escape hatch in the turret rear.

**Below:** A Tiger I heavy tank of the SS-Panzer Abteilung 101 moves through a French village in 1944. The Tiger I was a highly effective tank and could take on and defeat all Allied tanks deployed in the Normandy campaign, but its size and weight meant it was difficult to deploy over long distances.

**Left:** A patrol of the British Durham Light Infantry inspect a knocked out German Tiger I heavy tank during the battle for Normandy in June 1944.

**Above:** A British infantryman takes cover near a German Tiger I heavy tank knocked out during the battle for Normandy in 1944. This clearly shows the Zimmerit anti-magnetic coating on the Tiger I.

**Right:** A PzKpfw VI Tiger of the SS-Division Leibstandarte moves forward during the battle for Normandy in 1944. This had better armor and firepower than any British or US tank deployed in France.

**Below:** A German Army PzKpfw VI Tiger tank passes an Italian Army machine gun team, which is armed with a tripod-mounted 7.92mm MG 42 light machine gun.

**Right:** The crew of a German Army PzKpfw IV (on the left) stops alongside a PzKpfw VI Tiger during the battle for Normany in 1944. Both tanks are well camouflaged, as the greatest threat to German tanks came from allied airpower, which was highly effective in daylight. German tanks could only move for long distances at night or in bad weather.

**Below:** The turret of the PzKpfw VI Tiger II heavy tank was very narrow, in order to present the smallest possible target to the enemy.

**Right:** The German tank crews were considered to be the cream of the German Army, and had very distinctive uniforms. This is a selection of typical uniforms plus personal items, such as caps, helmets, and headphones.

**Right:** PzKpfw VI Tiger II with the more usual Henschel turret, which provided the maximum possible protection for the turret crew of three. The crew was made up of commander, gunner, and loader. The 88mm gun was fitted with a muzzle brake and was highly effective at long range.

**Right:** A PzKpfw Tiger II carrying Waffen SS Panzer Grenadiers during the Battle of the Bulge, the attempted German breakthrough in December 1944.

**Below:** PzKpfw Tiger II heavy tanks fitted with the Porsche turret. The vehicle was issued on the same scale as the Tiger I, but less than 500 were built.

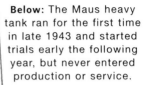

**Below:** The Maus heavy tank ran for the first time in late 1943 and started trials early the following year, but never entered production or service.

**Left:** A Maus heavy tank during trials without its main armament of one 128mm gun fitted. Most of the prototypes were blown up at the end of the Second World War, but at least one survived, and this one is now in a Russian museum near Moscow.

# *Profile:* GERMANY: Leopard 1

The German Krauss-Maffei Leopard 1 tank was originally developed to meet the requirements of the German Army, with the first production vehicles completed in 1965. Production ran through to 1979, but was subsequently restarted for the export market. The Leopard 1 rapidly became the most widely deployed tank within European members of NATO and sales were made to Belgium, Canada, Denmark, Greece, Italy, Netherlands, Norway, and Turkey. Australia also purchased the Leopard 1, and recently surplus vehicles have been sold to a number of other countries such as Brazil and Chile. While all Leopard 1s retained the 105mm gun and the same MTU power pack, the vehicle was constantly upgraded with additional armor and a more advanced computerized fire control system, including day/thermal sights and a laser rangefinder.

**Left:** A Leopard 1A4 tank of the German Army with its all-welded turret being put through its paces. This was the last production model of the Leopard 1 series as the latter Leopard 1A5 was an upgrade. All versions of the Leopard were armed with the British 105mm L7 rifled tank gun, with a 7.62mm co-axial and 7.62mm anti-aircraft machine gun.

Leopard 1A4 with infra-red searchlight over 105 mm gun.

**Below:** One of the more unusual Leopard 1s was this artillery observation post vehicle, which never entered production and had the 105mm gun removed.

## SPECIFICATIONS

| | |
|---|---|
| Nationality | German |
| Armor | classified |
| Combat weight | 93,400lb |
| Length/width | 31ft 4in / 10ft 8in |
| Engine | MTU MB 838 Ca M-500 diesel |
| Number built | 250 (Leopard 1A4s for the German Army) |
| 1st prototype run | 1960 |

**Left:** The Leopard 1A5 was an upgraded Leopard 1 with additional armor protection, especially to the turret, and a new computerized fire control system (FCS). The 105mm gun has a thermal sleeve and fume extractor. The Leopard 1 saw combat in the Balkans and is still widely deployed.

**Below:** The Gepard twin 35mm self-propelled anti-aircraft gun system is based on a modified Leopard 1 chassis and remains in service with Germany and The Netherlands. It is armed with twin 35mm cannon, computerized FCS, and tracking and surveillance radars.

**Left:** To support the Leopard 1 tank a whole family of vehicles was developed, either on the same chassis or new chassis incorporating the same components. These included armored recovery vehicles, armored engineer vehicles, and this armored launched bridge, shown here launching its two-part bridge over the front of the vehicle. In 2003, this was still in front-line service with the German Army and also used by other countries.

**Left:** The latest Leopard 2 has many improvements, including a new armor package providing greater protection, with the turret front having a distinctive arrow-head shape. The Leopard 2A6 also features a longer barrel 120mm gun, which increases the effective range of the vehicle by 1,000yd.

**Below:** Standard Leopard 2 tank having its turret removed by an armored recovery vehicle. This photograph shows the turret basket, which has seats for the commander, gunner, and loader. Ready-use ammunition is stowed in the turret bustle.

**Left:** Two German Army Leopard 2 tanks put through their paces. The Leopard 2 is armed with a 120mm smooth bore gun, which fires ammunition with a semi-combustable cartridge case. With the end of the Cold War, many German Leopard 2s became surplus to requirements and quantities were sold to a number of countries such as Austria, Denmark, Finland, Norway, and Poland. The Leopard 2 has become the most widely deployed type in NATO.

**Left:** The chassis of the Marder 1 infantry fighting vehicle was used as the basis for the TH 301. This model is fitted with a French FL-20 oscillating turret, armed with a 105mm gun. This combination underwent extensive trials, but never passed the prototype stage.

**Above:** The TH 301 tank was developed by Rheinmetall Landsysteme of Germany as a further stage of the TAM tank developed to meet the requirements of Argentina. It was renamed the R 301, and had a 105mm gun coupled to a computerized fire control system. It never entered production.

**Above:** The Indian Arjun tank has been under development for over 20 years and has been plagued by problems. A first production batch is now being built.

**Right:** The turret of the Indian Arjun tank is similar to the original production German Leopard 2, but is armed with a 120mm rifled tank gun with 7.62mm co-axial machine gun.

**Left:** The VFM 5 light tank was armed with a 105mm gun and 7.62mm co-axial machine gun, and fitted with a computerized fire control system to enable it to engage targets with a high first round hit probability while moving or stationary. Although demonstrated to a number of customers, it never entered production or service.

**Below:** One of the more recent light tanks is this ASCOD 105, in production for Austria and Spain as an infantry fighting vehicle. It has a South African turret armed with a 105mm gun and 7.62mm machine gun. In 2003, it remained at the prototype stage.

**Left:** Another international development that remained at the prototype stage was the VFM 5 light tank, which was a joint development for the export market by Vickers Defence Systems of the UK and the FMC Corporation of the US. The UK was responsible for the turret and the US company for the chassis.

**Right:** The Defense Industrials Organization of Iran has developed its own main battle tank called the Zulfiqar, which is armed with a 125mm gun fed by an automatic loader. Few firm details of this tank have so far been released.

**Right:** The Iranian T-72Z MBT is an upgraded Russian T-54/T-55 or Chinese Type 59 tank with its original 100mm gun replaced by a 105mm gun.

**Below:** Iranian Zulfiqar with turret traversed to the rear, showing suspension detail.

**Left:** T-54/T-55 tank of the Iraqi Army captured during Desert Storm, the recapture of Kuwait, in February 1991, and fitted with additional armor protection over the frontal arc.

**Above:** Iraq converted a number of surplus T-54/T-55s into specialized support vehicles, such as this 160mm breech loaded mortar, believed to have been produced in small numbers.

# *Profile:* ISRAEL: Upgraded Sherman

At the end of the Second World War, Israel managed to obtain a variety of surplus tanks from many sources, and of these the Sherman became the backbone of its armored units until the arrival of the British Centurion. The Sherman was upgraded in many areas, including the installation of a modified French 105mm gun and a new powerpack. Many Sherman tanks were also converted into specialized support vehicles, such as ambulances, observation post vehicles, and self-propelled guns.

**Below left:** The Soltam Systems 155mm L33 self-propelled gun was based on a modified Sherman chassis. It first saw combat in the 1973 Middle East conflict.

**Below:** This Sherman tank has been converted into an engineer vehicle by Israel, with a large, hydraulically operated dozer blade being mounted at the front of the hull.

The most sophisticated of all of the Israel Sherman upgrades was the M51 base, which was fitted with a modified French 105mm D1504 rifled gun and muzzle brake. This was fitted in a much modified Sherman turret with a new mantlet to take the larger caliber gun. The complete drive line was upgraded and a new Cummins engine was installed, increasing the combat weight to 39 tonnes. The vehicle first saw combat in 1967, but has now been phased out of front-line service. Some were subsequently sold to Chile.

**Left:** To make up for lost vehicles, Israel took into service many captured Russian-built T-54/T-55 tanks armed with 100mm guns, as shown here. These were, however, soon rebuilt and enhanced in many areas, including the installation of a 105mm gun and an improved fire control system. Many of the smaller sub-systems were also enhanced or replaced, as the original vehicles was not considered to be very good ergonomically.

**Left:** Under the leadership of Israel Military Industries, the US-designed and built M60 series has been upgraded for the export market to an enhanced version called the Sabra. Improvements include a 120mm smooth bore gun, computerized fire control system, and an enhanced armor package.

**Right:** Israel has captured large numbers of T-54/T-55s and many have been converted into heavily armored Achzarit armored personnel carriers, such as this one, which have seen considerable action in recent years.

The Israel Defense Forces took delivery of a large number of Centurion tanks from a number of countries, including the Netherlands and the UK. These were rebuilt and all were fitted with a 105mm rifled tank gun, a new fire control system, and the original gasoline engine was replaced by a more fuel-efficient US Teledyne Continental Motors diesel engine, which was similar to the one used in US supplied tanks. Later, the Centurion was fitted with locally developed explosive reactive armor to provide a higher level of protection against anti-tank guided missiles fitted with a high explosive anti-tank (HEAT) warhead. The Centurion gun tank has now been phased out of service with the Israel Defense Force, and most have been converted into vehicles with more specialized roles.

**Above:** Israel converted a number of Centurion gun tanks into this very well-protected Nagmachon heavy armored personnel carrier.

**Right:** The Puma combat engineer vehicle is based on a modified Centurion chassis, and is highly protected against anti-tank weapons and mines.

## SPECIFICATIONS

| | |
|---|---|
| Nationality | Israel |
| Armor | classified |
| Combat weight | 118,000lb |
| Length/width | 24ft 9in / 11ft 1in |
| Engine | AVDS-1790-2C diesel |
| Number built | classified |
| 1st prototype run | 1967 |

**Above:** This is another Centurion converted to an armored personnel carrier, with additional passive armor and remote controlled roof-mounted machine guns.

# Profile: ISRAEL: Merkava

Combat experience by the Israel Defense Force in the 1967 Middle East conflict showed up numerous shortcomings with foreign supplied tanks, such as the Centurion, M48, and M60, especially in the key area of survivability. By that time Israel had considerable experience in upgrading MBTs, and the logical step was to design a tank from scratch. The first prototype was completed as the Merkava in 1974, and, following trials, first deliveries of production vehicles were made in 1979. The overall layout of the Merkava is different from other tanks with powerpack at the front, and the turret and crew compartment at the rear. This has allowed the frontal arc of the Merkava to have the highest level of protection.

**Above right:** The Merkava Mk 4 is the latest version to enter production and has many improvements, including a more powerful engine, and new armor system.

**Right:** The Merkava Mk 2 is armed with a 105mm gun, also standard on Israel M48 and M60 series upgraded tanks.

**Opposite page:** The Merkava Mk 3 was the first model fitted with the Israel Military Industries 120mm smooth bore gun, complete with thermal sleeve and fume extractor. It also has improved armor, and a new computerized fire control system.

**SPECIFICATIONS (MK 3)**

| | | | | | |
|---|---|---|---|---|---|
| Nationality | Israel | Combat weight | 143,330lb | Number built | classified |
| Armor | classified | Length/width | 29ft 7in / 12ft 3in | 1st prototype run | 1985 (unconfirmed) |
| | | Engine | AVDS-1790-9AR diesel | | |

**Left and far right:** The first prototype of the Italian FIAT 2000 heavy tank was completed in late 1918, but never saw combat. Another four were built and these remained in service until 1934.

**Below:** The FIAT 3000 light tank was based on the French Renault FT-17 light tank. The first prototype was completed in 1920 and entered service with the Italian Army three years later.

**Below:** Italian Carro Armato M 13/40 medium tank, No 1, 3rd Platoon, 2nd Company, XI Battalion, which is now preserved as a memorial to the Italians killed at the Battle of El Alamein.

**Right:** The Italian Carro Veloce CV33 tankette had a crew of two and was armed with twin 8mm FIAT Model 18/35 machine guns. The SPA CV3 four-cylinder gasoline engine was at the rear of the hull. Fitted above this is a mount for an anti-aircraft machine gun.

**Right:** Reconnaissance version of the Italian Carro Veloce CV33 tankette shows how small these vehicles were and how cramped the crew of two must have been inside. Later versions have more powerful armament, and there were a number of specialized versions such as a flamethrower.

**Left:** British officers examine an Italian Carro Armato M 13/40 medium tank while its Italian crew look on. Some of these tanks were taken into Australian and British Army service to replace lost British vehicles.

**Above:** The Italian Carro Armato L6/40 light tank was developed in the mid-1930s, and over 280 vehicles were subsequently built.

**Right:** The Italian Army has recently taken delivery of 200 of these Ariete main battle tanks armed with a 120mm smooth bore gun. These have replaced many of the older Leopard 1 series tanks.

**Below:** OF-40 MBT showing its obstacle-climbing capabilities at the Oto Melara facility at La Spezia, where all Italian tracked armored fighting vehicles and artillery systems are manufactured.

**Above:** The OF-40 main battle tank was developed by the Italian companies of Oto Melara and FIAT specifically for the export market. It has a chassis and turret of all-welded steel armor. Main armament comprised a 105mm gun coupled to a computerized day/night fire control system. A total of 36 were built for Dubai, which also took delivery of a small number of armored recovery vehicles on a similar chassis.

# JAPAN, *SOUTH KOREA NORTH KOREA, PAKISTAN, POLAND*

**Left:** The Pakistani Army uses large quantities of these Chinese Type 69 tanks fitted with a 105mm gun.

**Right:** Japanese Type 89s series tanks parade through Manila in May 1942, clearly showing the hull-mounted 6.5mm machine gun and turret armed with one Type 90 57mm gun. There was also a 6.5mm machine gun in the turret rear.

**Above:** Japanese Type 89B tank as used in Manchuria and fitted with a special tail to assist in crossing trenches. The latter feature was copied from the French FT-17 light tank of the First World War. The crew of the Type 89B consisted of four men.

**Left:** Japanese Type 89B series tanks accompanied by infantry in China. This model entered production in 1934, with the original petrol engine replaced by a more fuel-efficient diesel that increased operational range as well as reducing the risk of fire.

**Above:** A US Marine takes cover in front of a knocked out Type 95 HA-GO light tank. Main armament consisted of one Type 94 37mm gun and a 6.5mm machine gun in the right side of the hull. Over 1,200 Type 95 HA-GOs were built, mostly by Mitsubishi. They saw service right through the Second World War.

**Right:** Top view of Japanese Type 95 HA-GO, with turret in centre of hull.

**Opposite page:** This particular Japanese Type 95 HA-GO light tank has had its Type 94 37mm gun removed and the position plated over for possible use as a supply vehicle.

**Left:** The Japanese Type 97 CHI-HA medium tank was normally operated by a crew of four consisting of the driver and bow machine gunner in the front, and the commander and gunner in the turret. Using the same chassis, the Type 97 CHI-HA was adopted for a wide range of other missions.

**Below:** A Japanese Type 97 CHI-HA drives down a road at Bukit Timah, Singapore, in 1942. After the end of the Second World War, captured vehicles were used by China for some years until replacement vehicles could be obtained.

**Left:** A Japanese Type 97 CHI-HA medium tank of the 3rd Company, 7th Tank Regiment, advances through the jungle on the Bataan peninsula during the invasion of the Philippines in 1942. Note the bank of smoke grenade launchers mounted on the turret roof above the 37mm gun, and the radio antenna that extended around the turret for improved reception.

**Left:** The first locally designed and built tank to enter service with the Japanese Ground Self Defense Force was the Type 61 developed by Mitsubishi Heavy Industries. The first prototypes were completed in 1957, with the first production tanks following in 1962. A total of 500 tanks were built, but it has now been phased out of front-line service. It is armed with a 90mm gun, with a 7.62mm machine gun mounted co-axial, and a 12.7mm for anti-aircraft defense.

**Above:** One of the more unusual Japanese tanks of the Second World War was this Type 2 KA-MI amphibious tank. It was basically a Type 95 light tank with a redesigned hull, fitted with large pontoons front and rear to provide additional buoyancy. When afloat, the vehicle was moved forward by two propellers and steered by two rudders. On reaching firm ground, the pontoons would be discarded and the Type 95 would advance inland as normal.

**Below:** The second locally designed and built tank to enter service with the Japanese Ground Self Defense Force was the Type 74 main battle tank, armed with a stabilized 105mm gun. The first production vehicles were completed in 1975 and over 800 were built. Like all recent Japanese military vehicles, it was never exported.

**Left:** The latest tank to enter service with the Japanese Ground Self-Defense Force is this Mitsubishi Type 90 MBT, which is armed with a 120mm smooth bore gun, allowing the crew to be reduced to three men—commander, gunner, and loader. The Type 90 can also be fitted with a front-mounted dozer blade or mine clearing rollers. There are also a number of more specialized versions, such as armored recovery vehicle, and bridgelayer.

**Right:** The Japanese Type 74 main battle tank has a number of unusual features, including a hydropneumatic suspension system which is operated by the driver. This allows him to tilt the tank left or right, forwards or backwards, and adjust the height of the vehicle to suit the type of terrain being crossed. There are a number of variants of the Type 74, including a twin 35mm self-propelled anti-aircraft gun system and a recovery vehicle.

**Left:** The latest production Republic of Korea K1A1 main battle tank is armed with a 120mm smooth bore gun, which is the US M256 manufactured under license.

**Above:** The first version of the Republic of Korea K1 MBT was armed with a standard 105mm M68 rifled tank gun. The K1 was originally developed in the US by General Dynamics Land Systems.

**Left:** The Al Khalid MBT is a joint development between China North Industries Corp and the Heavy Industries Taxila facility to meet the operational requirements of the Pakistani Armoured Corps. It incorporates advanced armor and a 125mm gun fed by automatic loader, which has enabled the crew to be reduced to just commander, gunner, and driver.

**Below:** The Al Khalid MBT has a hull and turret of advanced armor, but for increased battlefield survivability, an additional layer of explosive reactive armor is fitted over the frontal arc to neutralize anti-tank weapons with a high explosive anti-tank (HEAT) warhead.

**Left:** This is the Chinese Type 59 MBT upgraded at the Heavy Industries Taxila facility to the most advanced Phase III standard, which includes the replacement of the original 100mm gun by a 125mm smooth bore gun that fires separate loading ammunition. It also features additional armor protection over the frontal arm, to provide a higher level of protection.

**Left:** The Polish Army fielded large numbers of these TK-3 tankettes, which had a crew of two and were normally armed with one 7.92mm machine gun. Numbers of these were captured by the Germans and converted for use as ammunition resupply vehicles or for rear area security where their thin armor was adequate.

In the 1930s Poland purchased around 40–50 Vickers tanks, which formed the basis of the locally developed 7TP light tank. First models had two machine gun turrets, but the final model had a Swedish turret armed with 37mm Bofors gun with a 7.92mm machine gun being mounted co-axial.

For some years, Poland manufactured the Russian T-72M1 series main battle tank under license. Further development of this resulted in the PT-91, which has been in service with the Polish Army since 1995. For the export market an improved version has been developed with a more powerful engine, SAVAN day/night gunners sighting, incorporating a laser rangefinder, and a new explosive reactive armor package. A number of support variants are also marketed, including an armored vehicle launched bridge, recovery vehicle, and armored engineer vehicle.

**Above:** The Polish PT-91 is a further development of the Russian T-72M1 MBT with many improvements. The skirt type device at the front is to help reduce dust.

**Left:** The latest Polish PT-91 main battle tank, clearly showing explosive reactive armor package to provide a higher level of protection over the frontal arc.

## SPECIFICATIONS

| | | | |
|---|---|---|---|
| Nationality | Poland | Length/width | 31ft 4in / 11ft 9in |
| Armor | classified | Engine | Type S-12U diesel |
| Combat weight | 99,970lb | Number built | over 200 |
| | | 1st prototype run | 1992 |

**Right:** Head-on view of the Polish PT-91 MBT, showing explosive reactive armor over frontal arc and 81mm smoke grenade launchers either side of the turret, which are coupled to a laser detector system as part of a complete defensive aids suite.

# 5

# ROMANIA, RUSSIA, SLOVAKIA, SLOVENIA, SOUTH AFRICA, SWEDEN, SWITZERLAND

**Left:** Russian T-64 tank with mounting points for explosive reactive armor, only installed in time of war or tension.

**Opposite page:** The Romanian TR-85 tank is similar to the Russian T-54/T-55, but has six smaller road wheels, distinctive side skirts, and extensive external turret stowage, including a large box on the left side and containers of ammunition for the 12.7mm roof-mounted machine gun. This model also has a laser rangefinder above the mantlet of the 100mm gun.

**Above:** The Romanian Army is now taking delivery of an upgraded TR-85 main battle tank called the TR-85M1. This has a number of improvements, including a French all-electric gun control system, additional passive armor, and a new computerized fire control system. The latter includes a new ballistic computer, a new sighting system, and a laser rangefinder. The 100mm gun has been retained, but a new all-welded steel bustle has been fitted to the rear. Banks of 81mm electrically operated smoke grenade launchers are also fitted and these are coupled to a laser warning system.

**Left:** Russian T-26 light tanks move forward in an attack, closely watched by infantrymen. The T-26 was a further development of a British tank, and some 12,000 were built between 1931 and 1940 in many configurations.

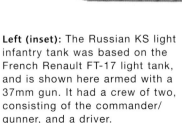

**Left (inset):** The Russian KS light infantry tank was based on the French Renault FT-17 light tank, and is shown here armed with a 37mm gun. It had a crew of two, consisting of the commander/gunner, and a driver.

**Above:** The Russian M2 light infantry tank was developed following the experience with the KS light infantry tank which entered production in 1928. Some of these were still in service at the start of the Second World War.

**Left:** The command version of the T-26 light tank was designated the T-26A-4V and could be easily identified by its all-round "handrail" frame type radio aerial. The vehicle has twin turrets, each armed with a machine gun. The T-26 light tank saw considerable combat in Spain in the 1930s, as well as during the Russo-Finnish War, and during the Second World War.

**Right:** A Soviet Army unit shows off its late production T-26 light tank, which has the more effective long barreled 37mm weapon. The hull-mounted machine gun has also been removed. Following their withdrawal from front-line service, many T-26 light tanks were converted to a variety of specialized roles.

**Above:** The Soviet T-35 heavy tank had a crew of 11 but was phased out of service by 1941.

**Right:** A Soviet T-28 medium tank had a crew of six and was armed with one 76.2mm gun and three machine guns. It was typical of tanks developed in the 1920s and 1930s.

**Far right:** The Soviet T-28 medium tank was captured by Finland and is shown here in Finnish Army winter camouflage. Although upgraded, the T-28 was replaced in production by the much improved T-34 series.

**Left:** Black smoke billows from a Soviet BT-7 fast tank as the driver revs up to lift his tank out of the water-clogged ditch. Main armament was a 45mm gun with co-axial machine gun.

**Below:** Soviet T-37 light amphibious tanks without their turret-mounted machine guns fitted and their tracks removed. It was in production from 1933 through to 1936.

**Below:** Soviet KV-1 heavy tanks operating outside Stalingrad during the epic siege of the city. The prototype was completed in September 1939 and production began in February the following year. It first saw combat in Finland. The KV-1 was well armored, and came with a 76.2mm gun and three 7.62mm machine guns.

**Right:** Proud Moscow farmers present the KV-1 heavy tanks they have paid for to their crews. Note additional fuel tanks mounted externally to increase the operational range of the KV-1. The vehicle was normally operated by a crew of five—driver and bow machine gunner at the front, and the commander, other gunner, and loader in the turret.

The Soviet T-34 medium tank is considered by many to have been one of the best tanks of the Second World War, and consequently it formed the basis of Soviet tank development for many years. It had good armor, mobility, and firepower, and was constantly upgraded and improved. With a well-trained crew it was highly effective on the

**Below:** The Soviet T-34 medium tank revolutionized tank design and the 76mm gun that was installed in early models was capable of penetrating and defeating all German tanks, with the exception of the Panther and Tiger.

**Left:** Soviet T-34 medium tanks on the production line. The first prototype was completed in January 1940 and full production started in June of the same year. By the end of the year, 115 had been built.

**Right:** The T-34/76B medium tank followed the T-34/76A and had a number of improvements, including a new turret of cast construction that was quicker and easier to make than the original welded turret.

battlefield. First models had a 76.2mm gun, but later production models had an 85mm gun, which saw extensive combat use in the post-Second War period in such places as Angola, Korea, and the Middle East. Even in 2003, there are still quantities of T-34/85 tanks in second line units in some parts of the world.

## SPECIFICATIONS

| | |
|---|---|
| Nationality | Soviet Union |
| Armor | 0.71–2.36in (18–60mm) |
| Combat weight | 70,550lb |
| Length/width | 24ft 7in / 9ft 7in |
| Engine | V-2-34 diesel |
| Number built | not known |
| 1st prototype run | January 1940 |

**Left:** T-34/76 medium tanks being loaded on railway flatcars at the Tankograd production facility for the journey to the front line, along with the crews, ready for action.

**Above:** Soviet T-34/76 tanks engage German armor during the Battle of Kursk. At one time the Germans considered copying the T-34 design, but eventually developed the Panther.

**Left:** The Soviet IS series of heavy tanks was developed in the Second World War. The first model was the IS-I. This IS-3 heavy tank was supplied to Egypt in the 1950s.

**Right:** The first IS tanks had an 85mm gun, but the IS-2 had a 122mm gun. By the end of 1943 over 100 had been built by the Kirov factory.

**Below:** The IS-2 heavy tank was well protected, with secondary armament consisting of a 7.62mm machine gun and a roof-mounted 12.7mm machine gun for air defense.

**Left:** The last Russian heavy tank to enter service was the T-10 series, armed with one 122mm gun, plus a 12.7mm machine gun mounted co-axial, and a 12.7mm machine gun on the roof for air defense purposes. It entered service in the mid-1950s but has now been withdrawn.

**Below:** The Russian T-62 MBT was armed with a 115mm gun and was first seen in public in 1965. It saw combat in the Middle East, but never replaced the older T-54/T-55 on a one-for-one basis.

**Left:** The T-10M heavy tank was a further development of the T-10 with the 12.7mm machine guns replaced by 14.5mm weapons. The 122mm gun has a distinctive mult-baffle muzzle brake. The 122mm gun was stabilized in both planes, and in addition to the high explosive and armor-piercing high explosive rounds, it could also fire a high explosive anti-tank (HEAT) round. Infrared night vision equipment was provided for the commander, gunner, and driver.

The Russian T-64 main battle tank marked a major change in Russian tank design, because the crew was reduced to three when an automatic loader was introduced for the 125mm smooth bore gun. Early vehicles had a number of technical problems that were eventually overcome. While the T-72 tank was widely displayed and offered on the export market, the T-64 was never exported and not shown in public. While few now remain in service with the Russian Army, large numbers are in service with the Ukraine. In fact, some of these have recently been upgraded to extend their working lives for a few years.

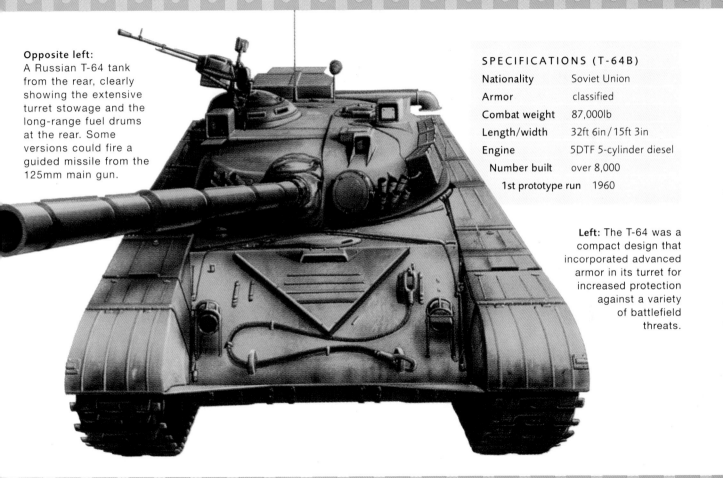

**Opposite left:**
A Russian T-64 tank from the rear, clearly showing the extensive turret stowage and the long-range fuel drums at the rear. Some versions could fire a guided missile from the 125mm main gun.

## SPECIFICATIONS (T-64B)

| | |
|---|---|
| Nationality | Soviet Union |
| Armor | classified |
| Combat weight | 87,000lb |
| Length/width | 32ft 6in / 15ft 3in |
| Engine | 5DTF 5-cylinder diesel |
| Number built | over 8,000 |
| 1st prototype run | 1960 |

**Left:** The T-64 was a compact design that incorporated advanced armor in its turret for increased protection against a variety of battlefield threats.

The T-72 main battle tank was developed in the 1960s as an alternative to the very sophisticated and expensive T-64. Various prototypes of the T-72 were built and tested before it was finally accepted for service in 1973. It entered service with the Russian Army in 1975 and was subsequently built in large numbers for the home and export markets. It was constantly improved with more powerful engine, better armor, and

## SPECIFICATIONS

| | |
|---|---|
| Nationality | Soviet Union |
| Armor | classified |
| Combat weight | 102,400lb |
| Length/width | 31ft 4in / 11ft 1in |
| Engine | V-84 V-12 diesel |
| Number built | classified |
| 1st prototype run | 1970 |

**Left:** Early Russian T-72 series main battle tank clearly showing the well sloped glacis plate which incorporated advanced armor. Night vision equipment was of the infrared type.

upgraded fire control system. The vehicle was also made under license by a number of countries, many of whom have developed the tank further in the areas of armor, mobility, and firepower. Further development by Russia resulted in the latest T-90, which is still in production.

**Left:** Standard equipment on the T-72 included an NBC system and the ability to be fitted with a snorkel for deep fording.

**Below:** Side view of T-72 series MBT showing long-range fuel drums at the rear, snorkel on side of turret, and gill type side skirts, which were designed to detonate high explosive anti-tank (HEAT) warheads before they penetrated the main tank armor.

**Below:** The T-72 MBT could ford to a depth of about 6ft without any immediate preparation. With the aid of snorkels the vehicle could ford to a maximum depth of 18ft with the commander giving directions. This type of operation was not without risk, and the river bed had to be firm with good ingress and egress points. Before these crossings, engineer units would normally carry out a detailed riverbed reconnaissance to see if all was well.

**Above:** A Russian T-80 series MBT fitted with explosive reactive armor over the frontal arm which provided it with a high level of protection against NATO anti-tank guided missiles.

**Right:** Russian T-80 tank with turret traversed to rear and showing the 125mm smooth bore gun which can also fire a guided missile out to a range of around 4,000m. This vehicle is also fitted with explosive reactive armor on the forward part of the turret, as well as on the roof.

**Left:** The T-90 series MBT is demonstrated to potential customers in the Middle East. The T-90 is a further development of the T-72, but with significant improvements in the area of fire control, night vision equipment, and new advanced armor package.

**Below:** Still at the development stage is the Russian Black Eagle MBT that has a bustle-mounted automatic loader.

**Bottom of page:** The Russian T-90 has been on the export market for some years, with the Indian Army taking delivery of 310 vehicles. Many of these will be manufactured under license in India.

**Left:** Slovakia is one of the many countries that have manufactured the Russian T-72 MBT under license, and further development has resulted in this enhanced T-72M2 with explosive reactive armor.

**Above:** The Slovakian T-72M2 MBT retains the 125mm smooth bore gun, but is also fitted with a 30mm cannon mounted externally on the right side of the turret to engage attack helicopters.

**Right:** For many years South Africa has operated a large fleet of Olifant tanks, which is the local name for the British-designed and built Centurion. This is the Olifant 1A that has many improvements, including a 105mm gun and a new diesel powerpack, which gives a significant increase in operational range. The Olifant tank saw combat in Angola during the 1970s, when it successfully engaged Russian-supplied T-54 and T-55 tanks.

**Above:** Many countries have upgraded the Russian T-55 tank, with the latest being the Slovenian M-55 S1. Developed with Israeli assistance, it has the original 100mm gun replaced by a NATO standard 105mm rifled tank gun.

**Right:** Other enhancements to the Slovenian upgraded M-55 S1 tank include a new explosive reactive armor package that provides a high level of protection against anti-tank guided missiles. It also has a defensive aids system that includes laser detectors coupled to the banks of electrically operated grenade launchers.

**Left:** Using its experience in the upgrading of the Olifant, South Africa then went on to develop this Tank Test Bed, which would have formed the basis of a new locally developed tank to replace the Olifant in service with the South African Armour Corps. The prototype was armed with a 105mm gun, but a 120mm gun was also developed.

**Left:** Further development resulted in the much improved Olifant 1B, which includes a new torsion bar suspension, diesel power pack, computerized fire control system, incorporating a laser rangefinder, and a passive armor package for the hull and turret.

**Right:** The Tank Test Bed had an advanced computerized fire control system that allowed the tank commander to track the target and then hand over to the gunner to carry out the actual engagement with the 105mm gun. The end of apartheid meant that there was no requirement to build a complete tank in South Africa, and so far the Olifant remains in service.

**Right:** The Swedish Strv m/41 light tank was a license-built version of the Czechoslovakian-designed TNHP tank with many modifications. It was armed with a 37mm gun and two 8mm machine guns.

**Right:** Another view of the Swedish Strv m/41 light tank, showing the hull and turret of all-riveted build.

**Below:** Side view of the Strv m/42 light tank, which entered service with the Swedish Army in 1944.

Between 1956 and 1958, the Swedish Strv m/42 light tank was stripped down and rebuilt to become the Strv 74 light tank. This has a new all-welded steel turret that was armed with a 75mm gun fitted with a fume extractor. A 7.62mm machine gun was mounted co-axial with the main armament and there was a similar weapon on the turret roof for anti-aircraft defense. There were two versions—the Strv 74H, with a hydraulic gearbox, and the Strv 74V, with a manual gearbox. The Strv 74 was eventually replaced by the Ikv 91 tank destroyer armed with a 90mm gun.

**Left:** The Strv 74 had a crew of four—commander, gunner, and loader in the turret, and the driver at the front of the hull. The Strv 74H carried 45 rounds of 75mm ammunition, and the Strv 74V carried 40 rounds of 75mm ammunition.

**Far right:** The Strv 74 fitted with a roof-mounted 7.62mm machine gun. The turrets were built by Landsverk, and Hägglunds and Soner.

## SPECIFICATIONS

| | |
|---|---|
| Nationality | Sweden |
| Armor | 1.57 in (40mm maximum) |
| Combat weight | 57,770lb |
| Length/width | 26ft/8ft |
| Engine | two Scania-Vabis Type 607 petrol |
| Number built | not known |
| 1st prototype run | 1954 |

**Left:** The chassis of the Ikv 91 tank destroyer was also used for experimental work. This is fitted with the two-man turret of the CV 9040 IFV.

**Below:** Together with the Centurion, the Bofors S-tank formed the main part of the Swedish tank fleet for many years.

**Left:** Main armament of the Bofors S-tank was a 105mm gun fixed in the glacis plate at the front of the vehicle. This was aimed by the driver, who raised and lowered the hull, and traversed the tank left and right to line up the gun.

**Below:** The Ikv 91 was armed with a 90mm gun fitted with a fume extractor and muzzle brake, and was fully amphibious.

'92 8

**Left:** One of the latest Swedish tanks is the Alvis Hägglunds CV-90120-T. Developed as a private venture, it is based on a modified CV 90 infantry fighting vehicle chassis selected by four countries. This has been improved and fitted with a Swiss RUAG Land Systems turret armed with a 120mm smooth bore gun. An advanced computerized fire control system is also fitted.

**Left:** The S-tank, showing 105mm rifled tank gun fitted in the glacis plate and an array of vertical bars at the front of the vehicle. These were a secret for many years and would have been fitted only in war. The idea was that the bars deflected anti-tank rounds before they hit the main armor.

**Right:** The Alvis Hägglunds CV-90120-T shows its low profile and its 120mm smooth bore gun fitted with a fume extractor and thermal sleeve. This fires standard NATO 120mm tank ammunition.

**Left:** A total of 390 Pz 68 series MBTs were built for the Swiss Army at Thun, and some of these were subsequently upgraded to the enhanced Pz 68/88 standard.

**Above:** This experimental Pz 68 has been upgraded in a number of areas, including the installation of a new armor pack for increased battlefield survivability.

# 6

# UKRAINE, UNITED KINGDOM, USA, YUGOSLAVIA

**Left:** A US Air Force C-130 Hercules aircraft with M551 Sheridan light tank being LAPSED (Low Altitude Parachute Extraction).

**Below:** The T-84 main battle tank is a development of the T-80 by the Malyshev Plant in the Ukraine, and is fitted with a 125mm smooth bore gun, advanced armor package, and a defensive aids suite.

**Right:** While Russian T-80s were powered by a turbine engine, T-80UDs built in the Ukraine were powered by a more fuel-efficient diesel. The latest T-84 tank developed in the Ukraine also features a very compact diesel engine.

# *Profile:* UNITED KINGDOM: MK I TANK

The stalemate on the Western Front during the First World War led to the development of a tank which was designed to cross the battlefield that was swept by machine gun fire and churned up by massive artillery barrages. There were also many obstacles such as ditches and barbed wire that could not be overcome by infantry. The tank soon proved its worth on the battlefields of France, but all too often the infantry could not be brought forward quickly enough to hold the

**Above and left:** The first tank to see combat service on the Western Front was the British Mk I, which was first used in combat in September 1916. The tank above is a Mk I (male), armed with a 6-pounder gun in either sponson.

## SPECIFICATIONS

| | |
|---|---|
| Nationality | Great Britain |
| Armour | 0.23–0.47in (6–12mm) |
| Combat weight | 62,730lb |
| Length/width | 32ft 6in / 13ft 9in |
| Engine | Daimler 6-cylinder |
| Number built | 150 (first order) |
| 1st prototype run | 1916 |

ground taken by the tanks. The British "male" tanks had 6-pounder guns, while the "female" tanks had machine guns. The crews worked in terrible conditions and many tanks were lost to German artillery, or simply became stuck in the mud of the Western Front.

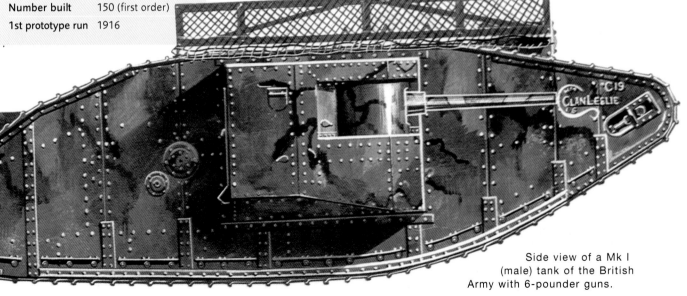

Side view of a Mk I (male) tank of the British Army with 6-pounder guns.

**Right:** The British Mk IV tank was considered to be the best tank of its time. This male version has side sponsons armed with a 6-pounder gun.

**Left:** To overcome the German trenches, British Mk IVs carried bundles of wood called fascines on top of their hulls which were then dropped into the trenches, allowing the tanks to cross without becoming bogged down.

**Below:** British Mk V tanks carrying special "Cribs" prepare to move up to the front line in September 1918.

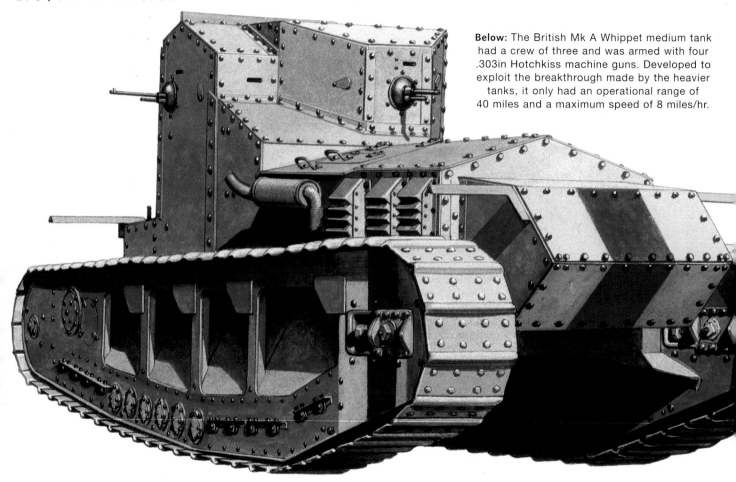

**Below:** The British Mk A Whippet medium tank had a crew of three and was armed with four .303in Hotchkiss machine guns. Developed to exploit the breakthrough made by the heavier tanks, it only had an operational range of 40 miles and a maximum speed of 8 miles/hr.

**Above:** The British Medium C tank combined the experience of combat of the earlier Mk IV and the Medium A (Whippet), but only a small number were built and it never saw combat service. These remained in service with the Tank Corps until 1923, when they were replaced by the Vickers Mk II medium tank.

**Left:** The Vickers medium tank was the first standardized tank to enter service with the British Army after the end of the First World War, and had a number of innovative designs including a fully revolving turret. This model is a Mk II.

**Right:** A Vickers Mk II medium tank showing its trench-crossing capability during a demonstration. This was developed from the Mk II, and was armed with a 3-pounder gun and three Vickers .303in machine guns.

**Left:** A11 Matilda I infantry tank from the rear. This had a crew of two and was armed with one .303in or .50in Vickers machine gun which was operated by the tank commander. First vehicles were completed in 1938 and 139 saw combat use in France during 1940, where most were lost. A few were used in the UK for training purposes. Further development resulted in the much improved Matilda II infantry tank.

**Right:** A13 Cruiser Tank Mk IV of 1st Armoured Division in 1940. This featured the US Christie suspension and gave the vehicle good cross country mobility.

**Left:** A troop of A13 Cruiser Tank Mk IV of 3rd Battalion, Royal Tank Regiment, patrol a road in East England during September 1940. Main armament was a 2-pounder gun and a co-axial machine gun.

**Right:** A13 Cruiser Tank Mk IV knocked out in Tobruk in May 1941. While the vehicle had a good turn of speed, its armor and firepower was lacking.

**Above left:** A column of "closed down" A10 Cruiser Tanks on the move. A development of the A9, the A10 did not have machine gun turrets in the hull.

**Above right:** The A10 Cruiser Tank Mk II was developed from the earlier A9, but had additional armor protection.

**Left:** The A9 Cruiser Tank Mk I had a main turret with a 2-pounder gun, and two hull turrets, each with a machine gun.

**Right:** A9 Cruiser Tank of A Squadron, 1st Royal Tank Regiment in North Africa in May 1940.

**Above:** A12 Matilda II Infantry Tanks of the Royal Tank Regiment in the Western Desert. This vehicle gave a good account of itself in the Dunkirk campaign, as well as in the early battles in North Africa, where its armor was sufficient against most anti-tank weapons.

**Right:** Two Matilda II Infantry Tanks being maneuvered by their drivers and showing the well-sloped armor. The arrival of the deadly German 88mm anti-tank gun meant the Matilda II Infantry Tank's days were drawing to a close, and many were subsequently converted into special roles.

**This page:** Drawings of the Crusader II (Cruiser Tank Mk VIA) in the markings of the 9th (Queen's Royal) Lancers, which was part of the 1st Armoured Division. Main armament comprised a 2-pounder gun with a 7.92mm co-axial BESA machine gun and a similar weapon in a small turret on the front of the hull to the right of the driver. The Mk III had the 2-pounder gun replaced by the more effective 6-pounder weapon. Over 5,300 of these tanks were built, and there were a number of specialized versions, such as close support, air defense, and a gun tractor.

**Right:** A famous picture of the North African campaign with British Crusader Cruiser III tanks on the advance. This version had the 6-pounder gun, with the hull-mounted machine gun removed. Note additional ammunition boxes carried on the front of the hull and additional fuel drums at the rear. Early vehicles had a number of automotive problems, but these were eventually overcome.

**Above:** An official cameraman films a Crusader I during the North African campaign. This vehicle has a Bren machine gun for air defense.

**Above:** Late on the first day of the Battle of El Alamein, a group of Crusaders and M4 Shermans advance against the Africa Korps. The nearest Crusader has a jettisonable auxiliary fuel tank at the rear of the hull to extend its operational range.

**This page:** Many British tanks were lost in the North African campaign due to mechanical faults rather than enemy fire. Here, a Royal Electrical and Mechanical Engineer (REME) unit loads a Crusader III tank onto a tank transporter under enemy fire.

**Left:** Valentine Infantry Tank Mk III during operations in North Africa. Vickers completed the first prototype on February 13, 1940, and named it Valentine. First vehicles had a 2-pounder gun, but these were replaced by the more effective 6-pounder on the Mk VIII model. Well over 8,000 were produced. Large numbers were also built in Canada, and most of these were supplied to Russia.

**Left:** The US-supplied M3 Stuart light tank was widely used by the British Army in North Africa and was nicknamed the "Honey," as it was so reliable. It was also used in the Far East.

**Below:** Disabled British tanks, including a Valentine in the foreground, litter the Western Desert in 1942. For the tank crews, the war was over, and the next stop was a POW camp in Italy.

**Below:** British Light Tank Mk VII (Tetrarch) was developed in the late 1930s, but only 171 had been built by the time production stopped in 1941. This Mk I CS (Close Support) Tetrarch was issued to HQ Sqdn, 6th Airborne Reconnaissance Regiment, 6th Airborne Division. It was flown to Normandy in a glider on the evening of the D-Day landings on June 6, 1944.

**Right:** The Valentine Mk V infantry tank leads a supply convoy in Tunisia, North Africa, early in 1943. This vehicle is towing a "Rotatrailer," with additional fuel and ammunition.

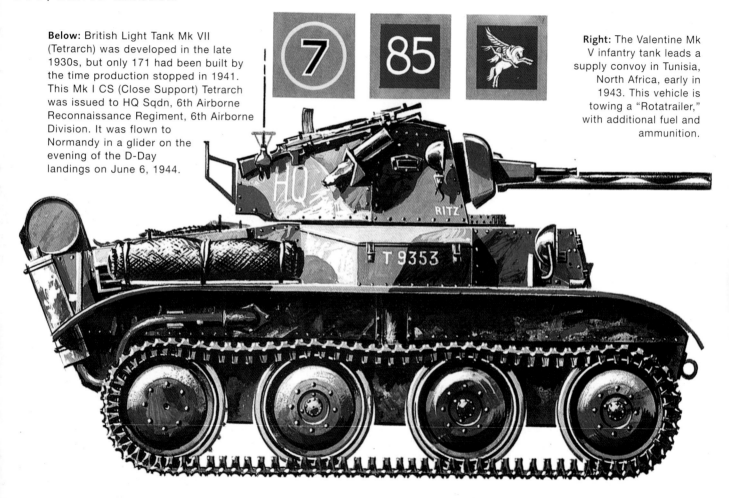

**Above:** An A39 Tortoise Heavy Assault Tank from the rear. This weighed almost 80 tons, and was armed with a 32-pounder gun and three machine guns, but it never entered production.

**Right:** An A22 Churchill infantry tank of the British Army's 7th Royal Tank Regiment, 31 Tank Brigade at Maltot, France in July 1944. This tank is fitted with the more effective 6-pounder gun.

# *Profile:* UNITED KINGDOM: A22 CHURCHILL

The A22 Churchill infantry tank was developed as the replacement for the earlier Matilda II, with design work starting in 1929 as the A20. The latter model never got past the prototype stage. Vauxhall Motors then took over, with first production Churchill tanks finally completed by mid-1941. Early versions had a 2-pounder, but this was soon replaced by a 6-pounder gun. It was also used as the basis for a number of specialized roles.

**Above:** Royal Tank Regiment squadron commander, second from left, holds an "orders group" with troop commanders on a Churchill III tank. The lieutenant on the left wears the correct pattern webbing and revolver for armored officers.

**Left:** The basic Churchill infantry tank proved capable of being adopted for a range of specialized roles, especially engineer vehicles. On June 6, 1944, one Churchill is being used as a bridgelayer, while the vehicle in the background (No 34), is a flail tank used for clearing mines.

## SPECIFICATIONS

| | | | | | |
|---|---|---|---|---|---|
| Nationality | Great Britain | Combat weight | 87,360lb | Number built | 5,640 |
| Armor | 1–4in (25–102mm) | Length/width | 24ft 5in / 10ft 8in | 1st prototype run | December 1940 |
| | | Engine | two Bedford 6-cylinders | | |

**Below:** Churchill I infantry tank with turret-mounted 2-pounder and hull-mounted 3in howitzer, which was removed from later production models.

**Above:** Crews of a British A27M Cromwell infantry tank take a rest in a field in France in June 1944. Their unit, HQ 22 Armoured Brigade, had been cut off for three days.

**Left:** British Army uniforms and equipment, including a Royal Armoured Corps pattern steel helmet, a beret with the insignia of the Royal Tank Regiment, armored crew denim overalls, binoculars, Pattern 37 compass pouch, first aid outfit, Royal Tank Regiment pennant, and Pattern 37 web gaiters.

**Above:** British Cromwell A27M infantry tank with driver's hatch and port (both open), and hull machine gun to the left. There is also a 7.92mm BESA machine gun co-axial with the main armament, which consists of a 75mm quick-firing gun fitted with a muzzle brake. Note the large rivets holding the additional armor on the turret in place.

**Left:** A34 Comet cruiser tanks entered operational service with the British Army late in 1944. The tanks featured a hull and turret of all-welded armor, armed with a 17-pounder gun on the turret.

**Above:** The A34 Comet cruiser tank had good armor, mobility, and firepower and continued in service with the British Army for some years after the Second World War. It also saw action in Korea.

Development of the A41 Centurion tank began in 1944. Six prototypes were built and sent to Germany, but they arrived too late to see any action. The Centurion entered service with the British Army 1949 and well over 4,500 were built, many for export. In British Army service the Centurion saw combat in Korea and the Middle East, and was eventually replaced by the Chieftain. Even in 2003, the Centurion tank is still used by a few countries, such as Singapore and South Africa. It had the ability to be upgraded in the areas of armor, mobility, and firepower as new threats materialized.

**Top right:** An upgraded Centurion of the Royal Danish Army showing a 105mm rifled tank gun fitted with a fume extractor but not a thermal sleeve, and enhanced night sight to the right.

**Right:** Upgraded Centurions of the Israel Defence Force armed with 105 mm guns advance on the Golan heights in 1973 during the Yom Kippur War. Israel has now phased these out of front line service, although many specialized versions remain in service.

**SPECIFICATIONS (MK 13)**

| | |
|---|---|
| Nationality | Great Britain |
| Armor | 0.8–4.6in (20–118mm) |
| Combat weight | 114,200lb |
| Length/width | 32ft 4in / 11ft 2in |
| Engine | Rolls-Royce Mk IVB 12-cylinder |
| Number built | 4,423 (all models) |
| 1st prototype run | 1945 |

**Above:** Early Centurion armed with a 17-pounder gun. Later versions had a 20-pounder gun and then the famous 105mm gun.

**Left:** Olifant Mk 1A tanks of the South African National Defence Force, armed with a 105mm gun fitted with a fume extractor, but no thermal sleeve. South Africa is one of the few remaining users of the Centurion tank in 2003.

**Left:** FV214 Conqueror heavy tank was the last of its type to be fielded by the British Army.

**Below:** During the Korean War, a Centurion Mk III armed with a 20-pounder gun, negotiates a temporary bridge built by US Army Engineers.

**Below:** A Chieftain armored recovery vehicle tows a Chieftain tank during a demonstration at Bovington, home of the Royal Armoured Corps. The Chieftain is fitted with winches and a dozer/stabilizer blade to carry out its specialized missions.

**Right:** The Chieftain replaced the Centurion tank in British Army service. The Chieftain is armed with a 120mm rifled gun that fires separate loading ammunition. Early versions had a 12.7mm ranging machine gun but later versions were fitted with a laser rangefinder.

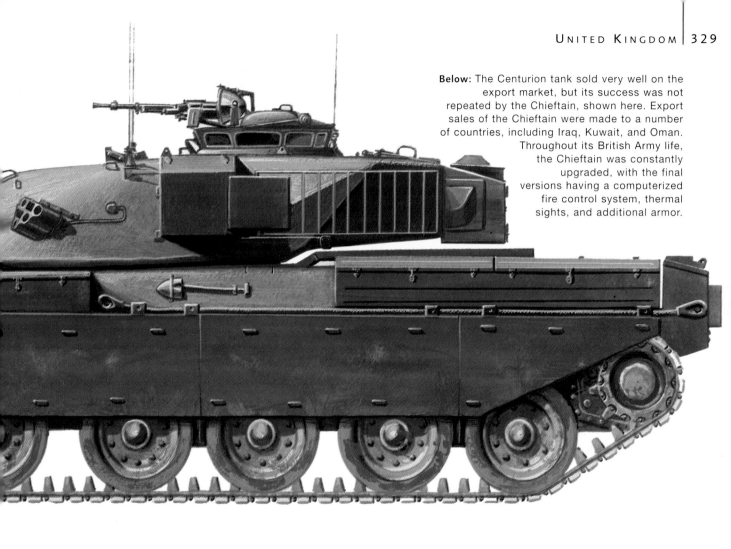

**Below:** The Centurion tank sold very well on the export market, but its success was not repeated by the Chieftain, shown here. Export sales of the Chieftain were made to a number of countries, including Iraq, Kuwait, and Oman. Throughout its British Army life, the Chieftain was constantly upgraded, with the final versions having a computerized fire control system, thermal sights, and additional armor.

**Above:** A Chieftain tank of the British Army with its turret traversed to the right to show its high level of armor protection over the frontal arc of the cast armor turret. The 120mm rifled gun is fitted with a thermal sleeve and fume tractor.

**Right:** When introduced into service with the British Army, the Chieftain was one of the best protected tanks of its time. It was, however, sometimes difficult to maintain and its engine was unreliable. It could rapidly be fitted with a front-mounted dozer blade.

**Above:** The Vickers Mk 7 was developed for the export market and was essentially a German Leopard 2 chassis fitted with a Vickers turret and 120mm rifled gun.

**Right:** Further development of the Chieftain for Iran resulted in the Shir Iran, which was eventually taken into service in Jordan as the Khalid.

**Above:** The Vickers Mk 7 was shown to potential customers, but eventually faded from the scene. It was the next step on to the Challenger 2 now in service.

**Right:** One of the prototypes of the Khalid tank undergoing trials. It was a late production Chieftain fitted with a more powerful engine, and is still in service with Jordan.

The Scorpion of Combat Vehicle Reconnaissance (Tracked) series of vehicles was developed by Alvis as the replacement for the Saladin 6 x 6 armored car. The basic Scorpion was armed with a 76mm gun, but subsequently a whole family of vehicles was developed and placed in production for the home and export markets.

**Below:** Two Scorpion vehicles, each armed with a 76mm gun, on patrol in Germany. The Scorpion was developed for worldwide deployment and could be carried in a C-130 Hercules aircraft.

**Right, above, and below:** For the export market the Scorpion was fitted with a Cockerill 90mm gun (above). The Scimitar (below) is armed with a 30mm RARDEN cannon and is still used by the British Army in 2003.

## SPECIFICATIONS

| | | | | |
|---|---|---|---|---|
| Nationality | Great Britain | Length/width | 15ft 8in / 7ft | |
| Armor | classified | Engine | Jaguar J60 4.2l gasoline | |
| Combat weight | 17,800lb | Number built | over 3,500 | |
| | | 1st prototype run | 1969 | |

**Below:** One of the prototypes of the Alvis Scorpion, armed with a 76mm gun and co-axial 7.62mm machine gun.

**Left:** A Challenger 1 with its turret being carefully lowered into position. A total of 420 of these were built for the British Army, but almost 300 have been passed onto Jordan, where they are known as the Al Hussein.

**Below:** The Challenger 1 saw combat service with the British Army in Operation Desert Storm, the recapture of Kuwait, in 1991. For this campaign, the Challenger 1 was fitted with additional armor over the frontal arc for improved survivability.

**Left:** A brand new Challenger 1 tank shortly after rolling off the production line at the then Royal Ordnance Factory in Leeds, UK. This clearly shows the high level of protection provided over the frontal arc and the 120mm L11 rifled tank gun fitted with fume extractor and thermal sleeve.

**Right:** The latest Challenger 2 tank being put through its paces. This will be the last tank to be built for the British Army, and is expected to remain in service until at least 2020 under current plans.

**Below:** A Challenger 2 fires its RO Defence 120mm L11 rifled gun during a night firing exercise. This model has long-range fuel tanks at the rear.

**Right:** The only export customer for the Alvis Vickers Challenger 2 tank is the Royal Army of Oman, which has taken delivery of 38 vehicles in two batches. These are to a different build standard than those of the British Army. They are also optimized for operations in the high ambient temperatures encountered in the Middle East. The vehicles retain the 120mm L30 rifled tank gun with a 7.62mm co-axial machine gun, and a 7.62mm machine gun for the commander.

Based on its considerable experience in the development and production of the Centurion and Chieftain tanks, UK company Vickers, based at Newcastle-upon-Tyne in the north-east of England, began development on a new and much lighter tank, which used automotive components of the Chieftain, but was armed with a 105mm gun. This eventually emerged as the Vickers Mk 1 that was sold to India—where large numbers were built under the local name of the Vajayanta—and Kuwait. Further development of the Mk 1 resulted in the Mk 2, but this model never entered production. The final production

**Above:** A Vickers Mk 1 tank fires its 105mm L7 rifled tank gun during a battle run in a demonstration for an overseas delegation.

**Left:** A Vickers Mk 1 tank armed with 105mm gun fitted with fume extractor and thermal sleeve. This model has a flotation screen that could be quickly erected to enable the vehicle to cross rivers under its own power.

model was the Vickers Mk 3. It retained the 105mm gun, but had a new turret design with a cast armor front for increased protection and a new powerpack built round the Detroit Diesel engine. Significant quantities of these were built for Kenya and Nigeria. A number of variants were built on this chassis, including an armored vehicle launched bridge, and armored repair and recovery vehicle.

The Vickers Mk 1 tank was developed specifically for the export market. It used the engine and transmission of the heavier Chieftain tank with the hull and turret of all-welded steel armor. Large numbers were manufactured in India for the Indian Army, where they remain in service in declining numbers.

### SPECIFICATIONS (MK 1)

| | |
|---|---|
| Nationality | Great Britain |
| Armor | 1–3.1in (25–80mm) |
| Combat weight | 85,100lb |
| Length/width | 32ft/10ft 9in |
| Engine | Leyland L60 multi-fuel |
| Number built | 2,400 (mostly in India) |
| 1st prototype run | 1963 |

**Left:** The last version of the Vickers Mk 3 was the Mk 3 (M) that was developed specifically to meet the operational requirements of Malaysia. It has many enhancements, including explosive reactive armor. However, it never entered quantity production.

**Above:** The Vickers Mk 3 was developed for the export market and featured a new turret with a cast armor front. This cast armor provided a higher level of armor protection when compared to the earlier Mk 1 with a welded turret. Armament remained a 105mm rifled tank gun.

**Below:** One of three T3 Christie medium tanks to enter service with the US Army's 67th Regiment, seen here with its fast, road running configuration. The tracks have been removed and stowed on the track guards above the road wheels.

**Right:** The US M2 Medium Tank had numerous machine guns fixed in its hull, firing forwards and all round the hull.

**Left:** The glacis plate of the T3 Christie was well sloped and carefully designed to defeat attack by anti-tank weapons.

**Left:** A British cavalry regiment, the King's Royal Irish Hussars, tries out its recently delivered M3 Stuart light tanks in the Western Desert in September 1941. These were widely used for reconnaissance, and armed with a 37mm gun, and a number of machine guns.

**Right:** US M3 Stuart light tanks at a US factory. Their main 37mm guns have been fitted, but they have yet to have their 0.30in machine guns in the hull and turret fitted.

**Left:** A US supplied M3 light tank of the British Army's famous 7th Armoured Division knocked out in the Western Desert in 1942. The vehicle had very thin armor that could be penetrated by German tanks and anti-tank guns with ease. Note the large number of penetrations in the hull and turret, resulting in the tank catching fire and being abandoned by its crew. Note also the extensive external stowage, as there was never enough room for all of the equipment required by the crew.

# Profile: USA: M3 Light Tank

The M3 Stuart light tank was developed in the US in the late 1930s and saw widespread combat use in all theaters during the Second World War and was continuously developed. While the M3 had good mobility, it lacked armor and firepower, and was therefore widely used in the reconnaissance role. It was replaced in production by the M5 light tank.

**Above:** Morning maintenance parade on a US-supplied M3 light tank of the British Army in North Africa.

**Left:** Australian infantry supported by Australian manned M3A1 Stuart light tanks advance on a Pacific Island.

## SPECIFICATIONS

| | |
|---|---|
| Nationality | United States |
| Armor | 0.37–1.75in (10–44.5mm) |
| Combat weight | 27,400lb |
| Length/width | 14ft 11in / 7ft 4in |
| Engine | Continental W-670 |
| Number built | 13,859 |
| 1st prototype run | 1939 |

Side view of Stuart Mk 1 light tank of the 8th (King's Royal Irish) Hussars at the Battle of Sidi Rezegh, November, 1941.

T.28078

**Below:** A typical sight from the Desert Campaign as US-supplied M3 Grant medium tanks of the British Army advance in February 1942. The main armament consisted of a 75mm gun mounted on the right side of the hull with limited traverse.

**Right:** A striking picture of an M3 Lee of the 8th Army, which belongs to the British Army 4th Queen's Own Hussars. The hull is of all-riveted construction, while the turret—armed with a 37mm gun—is of cast armor. On top of this is the commander's turret, with a 0.30in machine gun.

**Left:** An M4 Sherman medium tank of a Canadian armored regiment at Vaucelles, France, shortly after the D-Day landings in June 1944. The M4 Sherman had a high reputation for reliability and performance, but its main armament was not powerful enough to engage the German Tiger and Panther tanks used in the Normandy campaign.

**Below:** This was taken during training. A US Army M4 Sherman medium tank carries infantry, with the tank commander manning the 12.7mm M2 anti-aircraft machine gun.

**Left:** An M4 Sherman medium tank of the 1st Polish Armored Division, maneuvering on the Mulberry floating harbor off the Normandy beaches on August 1, 1944. Note the replacement track which is carried on the front of the vehicle, as well as the main gun and bow-mounted machine gun covered up since the vehicle was not going into immediate combat.

**Left:** British infantry on board an M4 Sherman tank in an orchard east of Caen, northern France, on July 18, 1944. The infantry would dismount before the objective was reached and then fight on foot with the tank providing covering fire.

**Above:** M4 Sherman medium tanks of the Free French Army's 2nd Armored Division in their marshaling area "somewhere in France" on July 21, 1944. Some vehicles have been fitted with additional armor protection to their turret fronts.

**Above:** A British manned US-supplied M22 Locust light tank (airborne) emerges from a Hanilcar glider during a training exercise. The M22 Locust was used in small numbers by the British Army during the Rhine crossing in March 1945.

**Right:** A total of 830 M22 Locust light tank (airborne) were built before production ceased in early 1944. Because of its light weight, it lacked armor protection. It came armed with a 37mm gun and 7.62mm co-axial machine gun. It had a crew of three—commander, gunner, and driver.

**This page:** The M24 light tank entered service with the US Army in 1944 and remained in service for many years. It was also supplied to many other countries, and saw extensive combat use in Indo-China by the French Army.

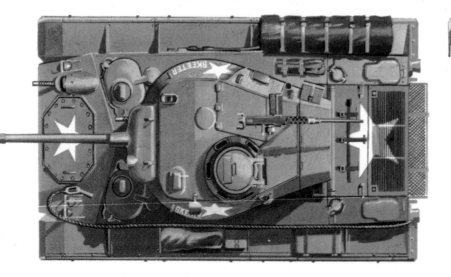

**Right:** A US Army M24 Chaffee light tank in Belgium, late in 1944. Its main armament comprised a 75mm gun, with a 0.30in machine gun being mounted co-axial, and a similar weapon in the bow. There was also a 12.7mm anti-aircraft machine gun on the roof.

**Above:** The close support version of the M26 Pershing heavy tank was designated the M45 and was armed with a 105mm howitzer. Only 185 were built and it saw limited deployment.

**Left:** The hull and turret of the M26 Pershing heavy tank was of all-cast armor sections, with main armament comprising a 90mm gun fitted with a double-baffle muzzle brake.

**Opposite page:** The US M26 Pershing was developed towards the end of the Second World War and saw action in the final days of the advance into Germany. It was also used in Korea, where it was the most well-armed and protected tank used by the US Army.

**Left:** This M41 light tank was upgraded by the Belgian company of Cockerill for the export market, with the original 76mm gun replaced by a 90mm weapon that could fire ammunition with enhanced penetration characteristics.

**Below:** A US Army M41 light tank on the ranges with spent 76mm cartridge cases on the ground. The M41 was replaced by the M551 Sheridan, but significant quantities of M41 are still in service in 2003.

**Left:** The US supplied large numbers of M41 light tanks to numerous countries and many of these remain in service today. Many countries have upgraded the M41, and this Brazilian vehicle has a new diesel powerpack, additional armor protection, and a new 90mm gun for increased firepower. Side skirts have been fitted to keep dust down, as well as providing protection against stand-off weapons.

**Left:** Large numbers of M47 tanks were built for the US Army in the 1950s, but it was soon replaced by the M48. The M47 was the last US tank to have a bow-mounted machine gun and a crew of five. Main armament comprises a 90mm gun fitted with a muzzle brake.

**Left:** The M103 was the last heavy tank to be deployed by the US Army and was armed with a 120mm gun. It was soon phased out of service, although it continued with the US Marine Corps for some years.

**Below:** An M47 comes ashore during an amphibious exercise. This M47 has a white light/infer-red searchlight mounted above the 90mm gun to engage targets at night.

# *Profile:* USA: M48 Medium Tank

The M48 was developed from 1950 onwards as a successor to the M47. The first prototypes were completed in 1951 and production began the following year. Over the years, large numbers were built for the home and export markets, with all production vehicles armed with a 90mm gun. Many of these were upgraded to the M48A5 standard, which upgraded to a 105mm M68 tank gun. Further development of the M48 resulted in the M60 series.

**Left:** M48 upgraded for the Hellenic Army, with a 105mm gun and new fire control system.

**Below:** Three 90mm armed M47 medium tanks of the US Army's 714th Tank Battalion in a night-firing exercise during Exercise Snow Storm in April 1953. After being withdrawn from US Army service, many were provided to friendly countries free of charge. A number of countries developed upgrade packages to include a more fuel-efficient diesel engine.

## SPECIFICATIONS

| | | | |
|---|---|---|---|
| **Nationality** | United States | **Length/width** | 28ft 2in / 10ft 6in |
| **Armour** | 0.5–4.6in (12.7–112mm) | **Engine** | Continental AV-1790-5B |
| **Combat weight** | 101,780lb | **Number built** | 8,676 |
| | | **1st prototype run** | 1950 |

**Above:** Germany upgraded a number of its US-supplied M48 tanks to this enhanced M48A2GA2 standard that had many improvements, including a 105mm NATO standard gun, and enhanced night vision equipment.

**Right:** The Israel Defense Force upgraded many of its M48 (right)/M60 tanks, including installing explosive reactive armor to the hull and turret.

**Below:** A scene in the streets of Hue in South Vietnam during the Communist Tet offensive in February 1968. A US Marine Corps M48A3 tank provides cover for a group of Marines who have come under sudden fire.

**Right:** A US Marine Corps M67A2 flamethrower tank, based on a modified M48A2 tank, attacks a Viet Cong position in South Vietnam early in 1966. Flamethrower tanks were widely used in the Second World War, Korea, and in South Vietnam, but they have long since been phased out of service with the British and US armies.

**Left:** The M60 MBT series was a further development of the M48 tank, with improved armor, powered by a more fuel-efficient diesel engine, and a NATO standard 105mm rifled tank gun. Although phased out of US Army service, it is still widely used throughout the world in 2003.

**Right:** An early production M60 clearly showing its infrared/white light search light mounted over the 105mm M68 rifled tank gun. The commander's turret is armed with a 12.7mm machine gun.

**Left:** The photograph clearly shows the all-cast armor turret of the M60A1 MBT, armed with a 105mm M68 series rifled tank gun fitted with a fume extractor. Throughout its US Army service life, the M60 series was constantly upgraded as new technology emerged. The final M60A3 were fitted with a computerized fire control system and thermal sights for improved target engagement.

**Above:** The early versions of the M60 MBT had a similar turret to the earlier M48, but were armed with the more effective 105mm M68 gun, which was the British L7 manufactured under license in the US.

**Right:** A US Army M60A3 MBT, with its turret traversed to the right, undergoing training. The commander and loader are both in the "head out" position. All M60 series have now been phased out of US Army service.

**Right:** The main armament of the M60A2 was a 152mm weapon system that could fire a Shillelagh guided missile or a conventional round of ammunition.

**Left:** Two production M60A2s during training exercises. The M60A2 was only used by the US Army and was not thought to be a successful design.

**Below:** The 152mm weapon system fired a Shillelagh guided missile, which could also be fired by the M551 Sheridan light tank.

**Above:** Mounted on top of the unusual M60A2 turret was the commander's cupola armed with a machine gun. The chassis was the same as the M60A1.

**Left:** The US Marine Corps fitted some of its 105mm armed M60A1 MBTs with explosive reactive armor to protect against anti-tank weapons with a HEAT warhead.

**Right:** The Egyptian Army has taken delivery of large numbers of new US-supplied M60A3 MBTs, as well as quantities of surplus M60A1s.

**Below:** The final production model of the M60 MBT was the M60A3, which had many improvements. For many years, this was the mainstay of the US armored battalions until it was replaced by the 105mm M1 Abrams vehicle.

**Above:** For trials purposes, the chassis of the M551 Sheridan light tank was fitted with the complete turret of the Cadillac Gage Stingray light tank.

**Right:** The 120S MBT was developed for the export market by US firm General Dynamics Land Systems and consists of a modified M60 chassis fitted with the complete turret of the M1A1 tank.

**Above:** The M551 was fitted with a collapsible screen around the top of the hull. When erected the vehicle was fully amphibious.

**Above, top:** An M551 Sheridan light tank firing a 152mm Shillelagh guided missiles during trials. It could also fire conventional ammunition.

**Right:** Another interesting vehicle developed for the US Army in the late 1970s was this High Survivability Test Vehicle (Lightweight). This was armed with an ARES 75mm rapid fire cannon, a 7.62mm machine gun mounted co-axial with the main armament, and a similar weapon on the turret for air defense purposes. It never entered production or service.

**Left:** In the late 1970s the US developed this High Mobility Agility test rig, which had a number of interesting features, including a high power to weight ratio and hydropneumatic suspension. Main armament comprised a rapid fire 75mm ARES cannon. The HIMAG was a test bed only and was never intended to enter production.

**Above:** The Cadillac Gage Stingray light tank was developed for the export market using many proven components and armed with a combat-proven 105mm gun coupled to a computerized day/night fire control system.

**Right:** For the export market, the US AAI Corporation developed this Rapid Deployment Force Light Tank, which is shown here being put through its paces during an overseas demonstration. It remained at the prototype stage and never entered production.

**Above:** The Cadillac Gage Stingray light tank armed with a 105mm gun was developed from experience in the design, development, and production of a wide range of 4 x 4 and 6 x 6 light armored vehicles. Most Stingrays were produced for the export market.

**Right:** Cadillac Gage Stingray light tank of the Royal Thai Army being put through its paces. To date, Thailand is the only customer for the Stingray with delivery of 108 vehicles. Further development has resulted in the enhanced Stingray II light tank, which remains at the prototype stage.

Following trials with two competing designs, the General Dynamics Land Systems design was selected for full development, and this eventually entered production as the M1 Abrams main battle tank. First production tanks were armed with a 105mm gun. This was followed by the M1A1 with many improvements, including a 120mm M256 smooth bore

First production M1s were armed with a 105mm gun, as were fitted to the early M60 series.

**Above:** A total of 2,374 105mm M1 MBTs were built and have since been phased out of US Army service. Many are being upgraded to become the M1A2.

## SPECIFICATIONS

| | |
|---|---|
| Nationality | United States |
| Armour | classified |
| Combat weight | 139,140lb |
| Length/width | 32ft 3in / 11ft 11in |
| Engine | AGT 1500 gas turbine |
| Number built | 610, plus M1 conversions |
| 1st prototype run | 1976 (XM1) |

gun, which is a licensed version of the 120mm weapon installed in the German Leopard 2. The final production model is the M1A2 which has many improvements, mainly in the areas of electronics, fire control, and protection.

The 105mm M1 Abrams tank was only used by the US Army and was replaced in service by the enhanced 120mm-armed M1A1. All versions are powered by a 1,500hp gas turbine.

US ARMY JE0001

**Left:** Manually loading a 105mm round into the breech of the M68 series rifled tank gun in the M1 Abrams MBT. This gun was also fitted into the earlier M60/M60A1/M60A3 tanks and is the British 105mm L7, built in the US with a locally developed breech mechanism.

**Right:** The 105mm M1 was followed in production by the M1A1, armed with a 120mm M256 smooth bore gun. A 7.62mm machine gun is mounted co-axial with the main armament and a similar weapon is provided on the roof for the loader. The tank commander has a 12.7mm machine gun.

**Left:** An 105mm M1 on exercise with turret traversed to the rear. Mounted above the 105mm gun is a device to simulate the firing of the 105mm gun while on exercise.

**Right:** The computerized day/night fire control system installed in all versions of the General Dynamics Land Systems M1 series of MBTs allows targets to be engaged while the vehicle is stationary or moving, with a very high first round hit probability. The fire control system includes a laser rangefinder to measure the range to the target.

**Left:** While the 105mm-armed General Dynamics Land Systems M1 has not seen combat, the enhanced 120mm M1A1 saw extensive use in Operation Desert Storm, the recapture of Kuwait, in early 1991, where it outclassed all Iraqi armor.

**Right:** A 105mm-armed M1 MBT moves forward with loader manning the roof-mounted 7.62mm machine gun. Once in action, the main role of the loader would be to supply the 105mm M68 series gun with the correct type of ammunition selected by the gunner.

**Above:** The General Dynamics Land Systems M1A1, with commander and gunner in the "head out" position. In combat the hatches would be shut and the tank sealed against NBC attack.

**Right:** One of the few versions of the M1 is the Heavy Assault Bridge (HAB) known as Wolverine. This is shown here extending its bridge over a dry gap ready for tanks to cross.

**Left:** The final production model of the Abrams M1 is this M1A2, which has many improvements, including the Commander's Independent Thermal Viewer, mounted just in front of the loader's position on the roof.

**Below:** The latest M1A2 is still in production for the US Army, although these are rebuilds of the older M1. The chassis is stripped down and upgraded. A new turret with the latest armor and electronics is then fitted.

**Above:** A clear view of the latest M1A2, showing the Commander's Independent Thermal Viewer, which enables hunter/killer targets to be undertaken under day or night conditions. The target is located and tracked by the tank commander, and then handed over to the gunner who carries out the actual target engagement. Enemy tanks are engaged using armor piercing fin stabilized discarding sabot—a tracer round which can punch a hole through any known tank.

**Above:** The United Defense M8 Armored Gun System was developed to meet the requirements of the US Army, but never entered production or service. It is armed with a 105mm gun fed by an automatic loader.

**Right:** An M8 Armored Gun System engaging a target during a firing demonstration while static. After the 105mm gun fired, the empty cartridge case was ejected out of the turret rear automatically and a new round quickly loaded.

**Above:** The Yugoslav M-84 tank was essentially the Russian T-72M1 series tank manufactured under license, but with many local modifications, especially in the area of fire control.

**Right:** The main armament of the Yugoslav-built M-84 tank was a 125mm smooth bore gun, fed by an automatic loader. This first loaded the projectile and then the charge. This enabled the crew to be reduced to three people. Note smoke grenade launchers either side of the main armament.

# INDEX

# PICTURE CREDITS

The publishers would like to thank the author, Christopher F. Foss, for supplying the majority of photographs
used in this book. Other images and line drawings are reproduced courtesy of Salamander Books Ltd.